SEPTEMBER 11, 2001

Pullis , Edward Francis (Teddy) Maloney , Edward J. Lehman , Edward J. Martinez , Edward J. Papa , Edward J. Perrotta , Edward James Day , Edward James White , Edward Joseph Mardovich , Edward K. Oliver , Edward L. Allegretto , Edward Lichtschein , Edward Mazzella , Edward P. Felt , Edward P. York , Edward R. Pykon , Edward Rall , Edward Raymond Vanacore , Edward Ryan , Edward Saiya , Edward T. Fergus , Edward T. Keane , Edward T. Strauss , Edward Thomas Earhart , Edward V. Rowenhorst , Edward W. Schunk , Edward W. Straub , Edwin J. Zambrana , Edwin John Graf , Efrain Franco Romero , Ehtesham U. Raja , Eileen Flecha , Eileen Marsha Greenstein , Eileen Mary Rice , Elaine Cillo , Elaine Myra Greenberg , Elena Ledesma , Eli Chalouh , Eliezer Jimenez , Elisa Giselle Ferraina , Elizabeth (Lisa) Martin Gregg , Elizabeth Ann (Betty) Farmer , Elizabeth Ann Darling , Elizabeth Claire Logler , Elizabeth Holmes , Elkin Yuen , Elsy Carolina Osorio Oliva , Elvin Santiago Romero , Elvira Granitto , Emelda Perry , Emeric J. Harvey , Emerita (Emy) De La Pena , Emilio (Peter) Ortiz , Emmanuel Afuakwah , Enrique Antonio Gomez , Eric A. Stahlman , Eric Adam Eisenberg , Eric Allen , Eric Andrew Lehrfeld , Eric Brian Evans , Eric L. Bennett , Eric Raymond Thorpe , Eric Samadikan Hartono , Eric Sand , Eric T. Olsen , Eric Thomas Ropiteau , Eric Thomas Steen , Erica Van Acker , Erick Sanchez , Erik Hans Isbrandtsen , Ernest Alikakos , Ernest James , Ernest M. Willcher , Ervin Vincent Gailliard , Erwin L. Erker , Eskedar Melaku , Esmerlin Salcedo , Eugen Lazar , Eugene Clark , Eugene J. Raggio , Eugene Whelan , Eugenia Piantieri , Eustace (Rudy) Bacchus , Evan H. Gillette , Evan J. Baron , Evelyn C. McKinnedy , Everett Martin (Marty) Proctor , Ezra Aviles , Fabian Soto , Faina Rapoport , Fanny M. Espinoza , Farah Jeudy , Farrell Peter Lynch , Faustino Apostol , Felicia Hamilton , Felicia Traylor-Bass , Felix (Bobby) Calixte , Felix Antonio Vale , Ferdinand V. Morrone , Fernando Jimenez Molina , First Officer Thomas McGuinness , Fitzroy St. Rose , Florence Cohen , Florence M. Gregory , Frances Ann Cilente , Frances Haros , Francesco Garfi , Francine A. Virgilio , Francis (Frank) Albert De Martini , Francis Esposito , Francis J. (Frank) Feely , Francis J. Nazario , Francis J. Sadocha , Francis J. Skidmore , Francis Joseph Trombino , Francis Noel McGuinn , Francis S. Riccardelli , Francis X. Deming , Francisco Alberto Liriano , Francisco Bourdier , Francisco Cruz , Francisco Miguel (Frank) Mancini , Francisco Munoz , Franco Lalama , Francois Jean-Pierre , Frank A. Palombo , Frank B. Reisman , Frank Bonomo , Frank G. Schott , Frank H. Brennan , Frank J. Koestner , Frank J. Spinelli , Frank J. Vignola , Frank John Niestadt , Frank Joseph Doyle , Frank Joseph Naples , Frank Salvaterra , Frank T. Wisniewski , Frank Thomas Aquilino , Frank V. Moccia , Frankie Serrano , Franklin Allan Pershep , Franklin Monahan , Fred Claude Scheffold , Frederic Kim Han , Frederick Charles Rimmele , Frederick H. Kelley , Frederick J. Hoffmann , Frederick John Cox , Frederick Kuo , Frederick T. Varacchi , Fredric Gabler , Gabriela Waisman , Ganesh Ladkat , Garnet Edward (Ace) Bailey , Garo H. Voskerijian , Garry Lozier , Garth E. Feeney , Gary Albero , Gary Bird , Gary E. Lasko , Gary Edward Koecheler , Gary Geidel , Gary H. Lee , Gary Herold , Gary J. Frank , Gary L. Bright , Gary Lutnick , Gary R. Box , Gary Robert Haag , Gary Shamay , Gavin Cushny , Gavin McMahon , Gavkharoy Mukhometovna Kamardinova , Gayle R. Greene , Gene E. Maloy , Gennady Boyarsky , Geoffrey E. Guja , Geoffrey Thomas Campbell , Geoffrey W. Cloud , George A. Llanes , George Bishop , George C. Merino , George Cain , George DiPasquale , George E. Spencer , George Eric Smith , George Ferguson , George Great Falls Simmons , George Howard , George Lopez , George Merkouris , George Morell , George Paris , George Patrick McLaughlin , George Strauch , Georgine Rose Corrigan , Gerald Atwood , Gerald F. Hardacre , Gerald Michael Olcott , Gerald O'Leary , Gerald P. Fisher , Gerard (Jerry) P. Moran , Gerard A. Barbara , Gerard Dewan , Gerard Duffy , Gerard J. Coppola , Gerard Jean Baptiste , Gerard P. Schrang , Gerard Rauzi , Gerard Terence Nevins , Geronimo (Jerome) Mark Patrick Dominguez , Gertrude M. Alagero , Giann F. Gamboa , Gilbert Granados , Gilbert Ruiz , Gina Sztejnberg , Giovanna (Genni) Gambale , Giovanna Porras , Glen J. Wall , Glen Kerrin Pettit , Glenn Davis Kirwin , Glenn J. Travers , Glenn J. Winuk , Glenn Thompson , Glenroy Neblett , Gloria Nieves , Godwin Ajala , Godwin Forde , Gopalakrishnan Varadhan , Gordon McCannel Aamoth , Goumatie T. Thackurdeen , Grace Alegre-Cua , Grace Galante , Graham Andrew Berkeley , Greg Joseph Buck , Gregg Harold Smallwood , Gregg J. Froehner , Gregg Reidy , Gregorio Manuel Chavez , Gregory Alan Clark , Gregory E. Rodriguez , Gregory J. Trost , Gregory James Malone , Gregory M. Preziose , Gregory M. Stajk , Gregory Milanowycz , Gregory Reda , Gregory Richards , Gregory Sikorsky , Gregory T. Spagnoletti , Gregory Thomas Saucedo , Gregory Wachtler , Gricelda E. James , Guy Barzvi , Gye-Hyong Park , Hagay Shefi , Hamidou S. Larry , Hardai (Casey) Parbhu , Harold Lizcano , Harry A. Raines , Harry Blanding , Harry Glenn , Harry Goody , Harry Ramos , Harry Taback , Harshad Sham Thatte , Harvey J. Gardner , Harvey Robert Hermer , Hasmukhrai Chuckulal Parmar , Heather Lee Smith , Heather Malia Ho , Hector Luis Tirado , Hector Tamayo , Heinrich B. Ackermann , Heinrich Kimmig , Helen Crossin-Kittle , Helen D. Cook , Hemanth Kumar Puttur , Henry Fernandez , Henry Miller , Herbert W. Homer , Herman C. Broghammer , Herman Sandler , Hernando R. Salas , Hideya Kawauchi , Hilario Soriano (Larry) Sumaya , Hilda E. Taylor , Hilda Marcin , Honor Elizabeth Wainio , Horace Robert Passananti , Howard (Barry) Kirschbaum , Howard G. Gelling , Howard Joseph Heller , Howard L. Kestenbaum , Howard Lee Kane , Howard Reich , Howard Selwyn , Hugo Sanay-Perafiel , Hweidar Jian , Hyun-joon (Paul) Lee , Ian J. Gray , Ian Schneider , Ignatius Adanga , Igor Zukelman , Ingeborg Astrid Desiree Lariby , Ingeborg Joseph , Inna Basina , Iouri A. Mouchinski , Ira Zaslow , Irina Buslo , Irina Kolpakova , Isaias Rivera , Isidro Ottenwalder , Israel Pabon , Ivan Kyrillos Fairbanks Barbosa , Ivan Perez , Ivan Vale , Ivelin Ziminski , Ivhan Luis Carpio Bautista , Jack Charles Aron , Jack L. D'Ambrosi , Jackie Sayegh Duggan , Jacqueline (Jakki) Young , Jacqueline Donovan , Jacqueline J. Norton , Jacquelyn Delaine Aldridge , Jacquelyn P. Sanchez , Jaime Concepcion , Jake Denis Jagoda , James A. Giberson , James A. Haran , James A. Oakley , James A. Romito , James A. Waring , James Amato , James Andrew Gadiel , James Andrew O'Grady , James Arthur Greenleaf , James Audiffred , James Brian Reilly , James C. Riches , James Christopher Cappers , James Corrigan , James D. Cleere , James D. Halvorson , James Debeuneure , James Donald Munhall , James E. Cove , James E. Hayden , James Edward Potorti , James F. Murphy , James Francis Lynch , James Francis Quinn , James G. Smith , James Gerard Geyer , James J. Carson , James J. McAlary , James J. Straine , James J. Woods , James Joe Ferguson , James Joseph Domanico , James Joseph Kelly , James Joseph Suozzo , James Kenneth Samuel , James L. Crawford , James L. Hobin , James Lee Connor , James Lynch , James M. Gartenberg , James M. Roux , James Maounis , James Marcel Cartier , James Martello , James Matthew Patrick , James Michael Gray , James N. Pappageorge , James Nelson , James P. Hopper , James P. Ladley , James P. O'Brien , James Patrick Berger , James Patrick Leahy , James Patrick White , James R. Paul , James Raymond Coyle , James Robert Ostrowski , James Sands , James Thomas (Muddy) Waters , James Thomas Murphy , James Trentini , James V. DeBlase , James W. Barbella , James Walsh , James Wendell Parham , Jamie Lynn Fallon , Jan Maciejewski , Jane C. Folger , Jane Eileen Josiah , Jane Ellen Baeszler , Jane Louise Simpkin , Jane M. Orth , Jane S. Beatty , Janet Hendricks , Janet M. Alonso , Janice Ashley , Janice J. Brown , Janice L. Blaney , Janice Scott , Japhet J. Aryee , Jaselliny McNish , Jason Cefalu , Jason Christopher DeFazio , Jason D. Cayne , Jason Dahl , Jason Douglas Oswald , Jason E. Sabbag , Jason Kyle Jacobs , Jason Matthew Coffey , Jason Sekzer , Jasper Baxter , Jay Robert Magazine , Jayceryll M. de Chavez , Jayesh Shah , Jean A. Andrucki , Jean C. DePalma , Jean Hoadley Peterson , Jean Marie Collin , Jean Marie Wallendorf , Jean Roger , Jeanette LaFond-Menichino , Jeannieann Maffeo , Jeannine M. LaVerde , Jeannine Marie Damiani-Jones , Jeff Mladenik , Jeff Simpson , Jeffrey A. Hersch , Jeffrey B. Gardner , Jeffrey Coale , Jeffrey Collman , Jeffrey Coombs , Jeffrey D. Bittner , Jeffrey David Wiener , Jeffrey Earle LeVeen , Jeffrey Giordano , Jeffrey Grant Goldflam , Jeffrey J. Shaw , Jeffrey James Olsen , Jeffrey L. Fox , Jeffrey Latouche , Jeffrey M. Chairnoff , Jeffrey M. Dingle , Jeffrey Matthew Palazzo , Jeffrey Nussbaum , Jeffrey P. Hardy , Jeffrey Patrick Walz , Jeffrey Randall Smith , Jeffrey Robinson , Jeffrey Schreier , Jeffrey Stark , Jemal Legesse DeSantis , Jenine Gonzalez , Jennifer DeJesus , Jennifer L. Howley , Jennifer Lewis , Jennifer Louise Fialko , Jennifer Lynn Kane , Jennifer M. Tino , Jennifer Mazzotta , Jennifer Tzemis , Jennifer Y. Wong , Jenny Seu Kueng Low Wong , Jeremiah J. Ahern , Jeremy Glick , Jeremy M. Carrington , Jerome O. Nedd , Jerome Robert Lohez , Jerrold H. Paskins , Jerry DeVito , Jessica Sachs , Jesus Cabezas , Jesus Ovalles , Jesus Sanchez , Jie Yao Justin Zhao , Jill A. Metzler , Jill Marie Campbell , Jimmie Ira Holley , Jimmy Nevill Storey , Joan D. Griffith , Joan Francis , Joan McConnell Cullinan , JoAnn L. Heltibridle , Joann Tabeek , Joanna Vidal , Joanne Ahladiotis , Joanne Flora Weil , Joanne Mary Cregan , Joanne Rubino , Joao A. Aguiar Jr. , Jody Tepedino Nichilo , Joel Guevara Gonzalez , Joel Miller , Johanna Sigmund , John (Jay) J. Corcoran , John A. Candela , John A. Cooper , John A. Hofer , John A. Schardt , John Adam Larson , John Andreacchio , John Anthony Sherry , John Anthony Spataro , John Armand Reo , John Ballantine Niven , John Bentley Works , John Brett Cahill , John Bruce Eagleson , John C. Willett , John Charles Jenkins , John Chipura , John Christopher Moran , John Clinton Hartz , John Crowe , John D. Levi , John D. Yamnicky , John D'Allara , John Damien Vaccacio , John DiFato , John E. Bulaga , John E. Connolly , John Ernst (Jack) Eichler , John F. Casazza , John F. McDowell , John F. Puckett , John F. Swaine , John Fiorito , John Frank Rizzo , John Frederick Rhodes , John G. Farrell , John G. Scharf , John G. Ueltzhoeffer , John Gerard Monahan , John Giordano , John Heffernan , John Henwood , John Holland , John Howard Boulton , John Iskyan , John J. Chada , John J. Doherty , John J. Kren , John J. Lennon , John J. Ryan , John J. Tipping , John J. Tobin , John James Badagliacca , John Joseph Fanning , John Joseph Florio , John Joseph Murray , John Joseph Murray , John Katsimatides , John Keohane , John M. Griffin , John M. Paolillo , John M. Pocher , John M. Rigo , John M. Rodak , John Marshall , John McAvoy , John Michael Collins , John Michael Grazioso , John Moran , John Napolitano , John Ogonowski , John P. Bergin , John P. O'Neill , John P. Skala , John Patrick Burnside , John Patrick Gallagher , John Patrick Hart , John Patrick Salamone , John Patrick Tierney , John Paul Bocchi , John Peter Lozowsky , John Robert Cruz , John Robinson Lenoir , John Roger Fisher , John S. White , John Salvatore Salerno , John Sammartino , John Santore , John Sbarbaro , John Schwartz , John T. Gnazzo , John T. Schroeder , John T. Vigiano , John Talignani , John Thomas McErlean , John Thomas Resta , John W. Farrell , John Wallice , John Wenckus , John William Perry , John Wright , Johnnie Doctor , Jon A. Perconti , Jon C. Vandevander , Jon L. Albert , Jon Richard Grabowski , Jon S. Schlissel , Jonathan (J.C.) Connors , Jonathan C. Randall , Jonathan Eric Briley , Jonathan J. Uman , Jonathan Lee Ielpi , Jonathan N. Cappello , Jonathan R. Hohmann , Jonathan Stephan Ryan , Jong-min Lee , Joni Cesta , Joon Koo Kang , Jorge Luis Leon , Jorge Luis Morron Garcia , Jorge Octavio Santos Anaya , Jorge Velazquez , Jose A. Guadalupe , Jose Angel Martinez , Jose Bienvenido Gomez , Jose Cardona , Jose Espinal , Jose J. Marrero , Jose Manuel Contreras Fernandez , Jose Nicolas Depena , Jose R. Nunez , Jose Ramon Castro , Joseph A. Della Pietra , Joseph A. Kelly , Joseph A. Lafalce , Joseph A. Lenihan , Joseph A. Mascali , Joseph Agnello , Joseph Albert Corbett , Joseph Amatuccio , Joseph Angelini , Joseph Angelini , Joseph Anthony Eacobacci , Joseph Anthony Ianelli , Joseph B. Vilardo , Joseph Calandrillo , Joseph Collison , Joseph Deluca , Joseph Dermot Dickey , Joseph DiPilato , Joseph E. Maloney , Joseph F. Grillo , Joseph Francis Holland , Joseph G. Hunter , Joseph G. Visciano , Joseph Grzelak , Joseph J. Berry , Joseph J. Coppo , Joseph J. Keller , Joseph J. Ogren , Joseph J. Zuccala , Joseph Jenkins , Joseph John Hasson , Joseph John Perroncino , Joseph John Pycior , Joseph Lostrangio , Joseph Lovero , Joseph M. Doyle , Joseph M. Giaccone , Joseph M. Navas , Joseph M. Romagnolo , Joseph M. Sisolak , Joseph Maffeo , Joseph Maggitti , Joseph Maio , Joseph Mangano , Joseph Mathai , Joseph Mistrulli , Joseph O. Pick , Joseph P. Henry , Joseph P. Kellett , Joseph P. McDonald , Joseph P. Spor , Joseph Patrick Shea , Joseph Peter Anchundia , Joseph Piskadlo , Joseph Plumitallo , Joseph R. Riverso , Joseph Reina , Joseph Rivelli , Joseph Roberto , Joseph Ross Marchbanks , Joseph Ryan Allen , Joseph Sacerdote , Joseph Vincent Vigiano , Joseph W. Flounders , Joseph Zaccoli , Josh Michael Piver , Joshua A. Rosenthal , Joshua Aron , Joshua David Birnbaum , Joshua M. Rosenblum , Joshua Poptean , Joshua S. Vitale , Joshua Scott Reiss , Joyce Ann Carpeneto , Joyce Cummings , Joyce Smith , Joyce Stanton , Juan Armando Ceballos , Juan Garcia , Juan Lafuente , Juan Nieves , Juan Ortega Campos , Juan Pablo Alvarez Cisneros , Juan Romero Orozco , Juan Salas , Juan William Rivera , Juanita Lee , Jude Elias Safi , Jude J. Moussa , Judith A. Reese , Judith Belguese Diaz-Sierra , Judith Florence Hofmiller , Judith Jones , Judson Cavalier , Judy H. Fernandez , Judy Larocque , Judy Rowlett , Julian Cooper , Juliana Valentine McCourt , Julie Lynne Zipper , Julie M. Geis , Julio Fernandez Ramirez , Jupiter Yambem , Justin J. Molisani , Justin McCarthy , Kaaria Mbaya , Kacinga Kabeya , Kaleen E. Pezzuti , Kalyan K. Sarkar , Kapinga Ngalula , Karamo Trerra , Karen A. Kincaid , Karen A. Martin , Karen Hagerty , Karen Helene Schmidt , Karen J. Klitzman , Karen Lynn Seymour-Dietrich , Karen Renda , Karen S. Navarro , Karen Susan Juday , Karl Henri Joseph , Karl Trumbull Smith , Karl W. Teepe , Karleton D.B. Fyfe , Karlie Barbara Rogers , Karol Ann Keasler , Katherine (Katie) McGarry Noack , Katherine S. Wolf , Kathleen (Kit) Faragher ,

Dept. of History, Columbia University
New York, NY 10027

Mae M. Ngai
Dept. of History, Columbia University
New York, NY 10027

Voices of Healing

Spirit and Unity After 9/11 in the Asian American and Pacific Islander Community

:: Editor
Icy Smith
Author of *The Lonely Queue*
:: Copy Editor
Marcie Dipietro
:: Editorial Committee
Christine Chen, Deborah F. Ching, Franklin Odo, Aryani Ong, Elizabeth R. OuYang, Icy Smith, Irwin Wong
:: Designer
Albert Lin

Published by the ⚬⚬ Organization of Chinese Americans and **East** West Discovery Press

This book made possible through a project by the Organization of Chinese Americans and donated to 1,000 libraries throughout the USA from the generous funding of the Ken and Karen Lee Foundation in memory of their cousin Betty Ann Ong."

Major funding is provided by 9/11 Healing Hands Fund and Cathay Bank.

Publishers:	Organization of Chinese Americans(OCA) and East West Discovery Press
Editor:	Icy Smith, Editorial Director, East West Discovery Press
Copy Editor:	Marcie Dipietro
Editorial Committee:	Christine Chen, Executive Director, OCA
	Deborah F. Ching, Vice President, 9/11 Healing Hands Fund
	Franklin Odo, Director, Asian Pacific American Program, Smithsonian Institution
	Aryani Ong, Director of Program Administration, OCA
	Elizabeth R. OuYang, Consultant
	Icy Smith, Editorial Director, East West Discovery Press
	Irwin Wong, Executive Vice President, Cathay Bank
Designer:	Albert Lin
Production Manager:	Icy Smith, Editorial Director, East West Discovery Press
Consultants:	Aryani Ong, formerly Nonprofit Consultant, Attorney; currently Director of Program Administration, OCA
	Elizabeth R. OuYang, Adjunct Professor, New York University Asian Pacific American Studies Program and Institute, and Columbia University's Center for the Study of Ethnicity and Race
Researchers:	John T. Akiyama, Consultant
	Clara Chiu, Director of Development and Outreach, OCA
	Corina Delacruz, Intern, OCA-Greater Los Angeles Chapter
	Alice Hu, Intern, OCA-Greater Los Angeles Chapter
	Juliane Ngan, Intern, OCA-Greater Los Angeles Chapter
	Aryani Ong, Director of Program Administration, OCA
	Elizabeth R. OuYang, Consultant
	Icy Smith, Editorial Director, East West Discovery Press
	Connie Sun, Intern, OCA-Greater Los Angeles Chapter
	Carolyn Troy, Intern, OCA

Disclaimer: The personal statements by the contributing writers in *Voices of Healing* do not necessarily represent the views or opinions of Cathay Bank.

This book project received permissions to use archival and research materials of AURA, Asians United to Raise Awareness, which also provided valuable technical support and consultation. Graphics and research were used with permission from AURA's "My America" concert, which took place in Manhattan on Sept. 8, 2002. Through the generous spirit of numerous performers, artists, documentarians, and volunteers, the "My America" concert commemorated and celebrated the Asian American and Pacific Islander involvement and heroism in the events of Sept. 11, 2001, and its aftermath.

Library of Congress Cataloging-in-Publication Data

Voices of healing : spirit and unity after 9/11 in the Asian American
and Pacific Islander community / Editor, Icy Smith.-- 1st ed.
    p. cm.
  ISBN 0-9701654-2-0 (Hardcover : alk. paper)
  1. September 11 Terrorist Attacks, 2001--Personal narratives, Asian
American. 2. September 11 Terrorist Attacks, 2001--Personal narratives,
Pacific Islander American. 3. Asian Americans. 4. Pacific Islander
Americans. I. Smith, Icy.
  HV6432.V645 2004
  974.7'1044--dc22

                                                    2003020028

ISBN: 0-9701654-2-0

FIRST EDITION 2004
Second Printing
Printed in Korea
Produced by East West Discovery Press
Published in the United States of America

FOREWORD

:: By Corky Lee
August 2003

I am a photojournalist, not a speaker or a writer. Putting my thoughts from ink to paper has never been a task that I relish. However, I can instinctively put film to camera, practice "photographic justice" and "serve the people."

Any photojournalist will tell you that one must cover the reaction to any news event as well as the actual event. In the aftermath of September 11, I photographed the human and physical void left by the World Trade Center. But I also trained my lenses and energy on a community of voices often not heard or seen- specifically Asian Americans and Pacific Islanders. Based in New York City, I have spent decades documenting Chinatown and its people. September 11 had a particularly devastating effect on Chinatown because of its proximity to Ground Zero.

I tried to capture the effect of September 11 on Asian Americans and Pacific Islanders as they contributed to the healing of open wounds. In the process, I was able to witness and chronicle the humility, humanity and patriotism of my fellow Americans who happened to have Asian and Pacific Islander roots.

Until *Voices of Healing* came to my attention, it was inconceivable to me that there was no record of the contributions, heroism and continued determination on the part of Asian Americans and Pacific Islanders to renew and rebuild their lives and communities after September 11. Along with the rest of the country, Asian American was shocked by the death and destruction on the East Coast. The ripple effects touched Hawaii as well. The writers and researchers of *Voices of Healing* could not cover every story connected to that fateful day, but the pictorial presented here provides a beginning for us to tell our stories.

Unimaginable situations were thrust upon ordinary people. They survived and emerged from the crisis as extraordinary individuals. Some will say they were "just doing their job." Others will convince you that they "had to do something or anything." Their actions demonstrated their patriotism as world citizens without any flag waving. This is the fabric of a great society. This diverse weave of people who call America home make it kind, generous, giving and strong.

Do not ever let anyone tell you to go back to the country of your ancestors. You belong here. Immigrants built America. It was created for you and me.

So turn the page, read on, be inspired, be proud, be American.

PREFACE

:: By Icy Smith
Editor
August 2003

The attacks of September 11 affected thousands of Americans. Among them were the hundreds of Asian Americans who were killed, and the thousands of workers and families in New York's Chinatown who were displaced. Many South Asian Americans and Muslim Americans suffered violent backlash and faced anti-Muslim sentiment. Yet, only a few of these tragic stories have been featured in the mainstream media. To promote a greater understanding of the effects of the September 11 tragedy on both human and civil rights levels, the Organization of Chinese Americans (OCA) took a leadership role in collecting photographs and writings from the Asian American and Pacific Islander community. With major funding provided by the 9/11 Healing Hands Fund and Cathay Bank, OCA and East West Discovery Press embarked on the mission of publishing this commemoration of the Asian American and Pacific Islander heroes and victims of the September 11 attacks.

During our research, we heard many inspiring stories. One was the rescuer Zhe Zheng, who was killed in the fallen buildings while volunteering his services as a certified emergency medical technician. Isaac Ho`opi`i, a Pentagon police officer, risked his life to rescue 14 people from the burning building. Ho`opi`i later learned that he may have made the ultimate sacrifice since his heroic feat exposed him to asbestos. And Robert Ideishi, a World Trade Center survivor, will never forget the countless acts of bravery and the genuine concern for fellow human beings that he witnessed that day. Through these stories, researchers and writers shared their grief and found fortitude and endurance.

Months after the September 11 attacks, Asian Americans and Pacific Islanders continued to experience the after-effects felt by all Americans. According to an economic impact study by the Asian American Federation of New York, New York's Chinatown suffered an unprecedented level of business, job, and wage losses. Chinatown's garment industry lost nearly $500 million in the year following the tragic events, with the number of garment factory closures rising to 65. Most of the nearly 8,000 Chinatown workers who lost jobs as a result of September 11 were still looking for work a year after the tragedy. Finding new jobs has been difficult for these unemployed workers, as many of them have limited work skills. In addition, the substantial reduction in wages imposed severe economic burdens on the existing Chinatown families who are living in substandard housing with incomes below the poverty level. Continued street closures restricted caregivers from visiting homebound seniors, goods delivery, tourism, and economic growth in Chinatown. The list of adversities goes on and on.

Despite these hardships and challenges, Asian American and Pacific Islander community groups called for unified actions nationwide to provide assistance to individuals and communities in New York City whose lives had been affected by the tragic events of September 11.

Two days after the attack, a local Chinese radio station in New York launched a fundraising campaign to assist the city's relief efforts. Within two weeks, the station raised over $1.45 million from Chinese communities across the nation to help support the American Red Cross and the Twin Towers Fund. In response to the crisis, Cathay Bank, a Chinese

American commercial bank headquartered in Los Angeles, reached out to help by donating $250,000 to establish the 9/11 Healing Hands Fund; they were joined by the OCA one week later following the attacks. Asian American and Pacific Islander companies manufactured American flags, and workers made patriotic pins with beads by hand, and donated the proceeds to the fund. To join these national relief efforts, community groups raised money during a week-long Chinese Moon Festival in October 2001, in support of the ongoing rebuilding and recovery operations in New York City. The outpouring of generosity, spirit of cooperation, and sense of community caring has been commendable.

Every voice in the community is full of a human spirit we all share. Magnificent solidarity emerges as never before from corporate leaders, to garment workers, and immigrants to servicemen who fight on the front lines. Their renewed spirit and strength show what holds us together as a nation.

On the other hand, problems remain. Ironies abound in the wake of September 11. Since the September 11 attacks, American Muslims, South Asian Americans, and many others perceived to be Middle Eastern have been subjected to harassment and violence. Asian American and Pacific Islander scholars expressed their voices on the ongoing crisis of war in the Middle East. Activists and various civil groups called for unity and civil liberties in the U.S.

Historically, in times of war or economic downturn, certain groups of Americans—because of their ancestry—have been adversely affected. For almost a century, Chinese Americans were made scapegoats for perceived economic problems. They were subjected to the racism institutionalized by the Chinese Exclusion Act for 61 years. During World War II, Japanese Americans were stereotyped as spies for the Japanese government. Without any proof of wrongdoing, 120,000 of them were interned. In 1983, a Congressional commission officially declared that the internment was not justified. The original cause of the internment was determined to have been motivated by "race prejudice, war hysteria, and a failure of political leadership."

As the events following September 11 continue to unfold, much is yet to be learned. We have realized once again what it truly means to be American! However, those not remembering the past are condemned to repeat it.

Through this community project, we are proud to honor these heroic souls with love and respect. *Voices of Healing* is a testament to the strength of the human spirit, and a call to the nation for healing and unity.

Note: Icy Smith is the author of the award-winning book, *The Lonely Queue: The forgotten history of the courageous Chinese Americans in Los Angeles*, and the editorial director of East West Discovery Press.

ACKNOWLEDGMENTS

The Organization of Chinese Americans(OCA) and East West Discovery Press pay tribute to all the victims of September 11, the heroes who prevented more tragic loss, and all who exhibited a healing spirit toward their fellow Americans in the nation's time of grief and loss. We also express support for people who experienced racial intolerance in the aftermath of September 11.

Without major funding from Cathay Bank and the 9/11 Healing Hands Fund, the birth of *Voices of Healing* would not have been possible. We are indebted to these organizations for their generous support of this publication. We thank Debbie Ching for her advice throughout the editorial process, and Irwin Wong and Heidi Wong for reviewing the manuscript.

We are grateful to the Asians United to Raise Awareness (AURA) Fund for its contribution to this project. We thank Franklin Odo, Director, Asian Pacific American Programs, Smithsonian Institution, for his assistance during the editorial process, and Helen Zia for allowing us to republish an essay that gave clear voice to our perspectives on September 11.

OCA expresses gratitude to Icy Smith, publisher and editorial director, East West Discovery Press, for elevating the level of *Voices of Healing* from its initial idea as an informal circular to a professional publication. She worked on the project tirelessly and played many roles, from editorial director and production manager to publisher.

We recognize Kathay Feng of the Greater Los Angeles-OCA Chapter for her role in discussions with Cathay Bank that led to the formation of this publication. At the OCA National Office, Aryani Ong managed the project with team members Christine Chen and consultant Elizabeth OuYang, and with the assistance of Carolyn Troy, Diana Yuen, Natalie Wong, and consultant John Akiyama. We are grateful to Clara Chiu, who led a research team including Aileen Chou, Corina Delacruz, Alice Hu, Juliane Ngan, Connie Sun, and Michelle Yuen to research photographs and contact information for victims' families. We thank Leo Lee, Georgia Lo, Ray Louie, Daphne Kwok, Frank Wu, and Jeff Yang for lending their support and ideas. In addition, we would like to thank the OCA National Office staff and more than 50 OCA chapters for their fundraising efforts for the 9/11 Healing Hands Fund.

Special thanks go to Marcie DiPietro for her dedicated and meticulous copyediting effort; Albert Lin for diligently producing this unique publication; and Gillian Dale and Michael Smith for their insightful advice on the project. Appreciation also goes to the freelance photographers who donated their outstanding work: Emmy Akiyama, Seshu Badrinath/Pipal Productions, David Bacon, Jim Barcus, May Chen, Violeta Chen, Jami Gong, Rick Ho, Chenghui Hsu, Hyungwon Kang, Synta Keeling, Corky Lee, Todd Leong, Yujian Liu, and J.K. Yamamoto. We honor Corky Lee, photo documentarian, for his continued service to the Asian American and Pacific Islander community, particularly in New York's Chinatown.

Many people gave generously of their time toward this project. We thank Manjit Singh and Preet Preemohan of Sikh Mediawatch and Resource Task Force (SMART); Meg Falk at the Pentagon; Marian Tan Johnson, Project CORE at the Coalition for Asian American Children and Families; Yujian Liu of *Coastide Magazine*; Charles Chung and Fanny Lawren of *Sing Tao Newspaper*; Monica Liu of *World Journal*; Lisa Phelan and Therese Gamba at KGO-TV; Betty Lam at the White House Initiative on Asian Americans and Pacific Islanders; Kevin Chapman at the Department of Transportation; Vicki Shu at Asian American Federation of New York (AAFNY); and Renata Huang for helping us reach contributors and procure photos.

Several community organizations gave us generous assistance. We are grateful to Asian Americans for Equality (AAFE); Asian American Federation of New York (AAFNY); Charles B. Wang Community Health Center; Chinese-American Planning Council; Chinese Consolidated Benevolent Association; Chinatown Progressive Association; Chinese Staff and Workers' Association; Filipinos for Affirmative Action; Hamilton Madison House, Inc.; Japanese American Citizens League; Japanese American Social Services, Inc.; South Asian Youth Action, Inc.; New York Taxi Workers Alliance; the radio station AM1480; and the Asian American Arts Centre.

The heart of *Voices of Healing* belongs to the families and friends of the victims, survivors, and eyewitnesses who shared their personal lives and stories with our contributing writers Aryani Ong, Elizabeth OuYang, Icy Smith, and Carolyn Troy, at the risk of reliving painful memories. Several of the personal stories were written by them. We thank the young people who gave us insight into their hearts and minds. We express gratitude to the writers and artists who shared their work to enhance this publication. We are indebted to all the contributors who gave their time to remember that tragic day, put their thoughts to paper, and document their stories through photographs. We hope for them a peaceful future.

ices of Healing

Ground Zero © Corky Lee

TABLE OF CONTENTS

INTRODUCTION

:: By Christine Chen
Executive Director, Organization of Chinese Americans(OCA), Washington, D.C.
September 2003

September 11 was a defining moment for America. People remember with painful clarity the events of that fateful day and their own reactions. Shock. Fear. Anger. Sadness. Patriotism. As the adage goes, the worst brings out the best in humankind. People wanted to assist the victims, their families, the New York Fire Department, and the residents of New York City who bore the brunt of terrorism on American soil. Millions of dollars were raised for victims' relief and emergency efforts.

In the same spirit, members of the Organization of Chinese Americans (OCA), as well as the Asian American and Pacific Islander (APIA) community, were seeking ways to assist with the efforts to rebuild the shattered lives and environment of the people directly affected and to join in the overall movement to heal a nation. On Sept. 27, 2001, OCA joined Cathay Bank in a national campaign called the 9/11 Healing Hands Fund to raise donations to rebuild America. Cathay Bank gave an initial $250,000 contribution. By the end of 2001, the fund had received nearly $400,000. The fund provided the Asian American Federation of New York (AAFNY) with support for its advocacy work on behalf of the New York Chinatown area, a site not far from the World Trade Center, which had been economically devastated by road closures and lost tourism that continued for weeks after the attacks. According to reports on the economic impact on Chinatown, AAFNY found that the garment industry alone lost nearly $500 million in the year following September 11. Further, it was estimated that upwards of $30 million was needed to provide job training and employment services for 8,000 dislocated workers. However, only $1.7 million public and private funds were made available.

The 9/11 Healing Hands Fund also supports *Voices of Healing: Spirit and Unity After 9/11 in the Asian American and Pacific Islander Community*. OCA, Cathay Bank, and East West Discovery Press collaborated to produce the publication. A majority of the copies of *Voices of Healing* will be donated to schools and libraries to educate the public on the history of APIAs and their connection to September 11.

OCA wanted to co-publish the pictorial for several reasons. The first is to depict Asian Americans and Pacific Islanders as Americans who, like all Americans, grieved the losses of life, celebrated the heroic feats of several kind-hearted people, participated in the relief efforts, and joined in the healing spirit of America rising to overcome an incomprehensible tragedy. Throughout the years, APIAs generally had been seen as foreigners, and not readily accepted as "true" Americans. Yet, the following pages will illustrate the stories of APIAs that resonate as strong as any other stories related to September 11. Take for example, Teddington H. Moy, a civilian program manager who perished at the Pentagon. According to his wife, Moy "loved his family, country and God." Every July 4 and Memorial Day holidays, Moy would dress from head to toe in red, white, and blue.

The second reason OCA wanted to be involved in this project is to tell the untold stories. Many APIAs and Asian nationals perished in New York, Pennsylvania, and Virginia on September 11. Eight thousand workers were laid off in New York City's Chinatown. Community organizations witnessed an increase in the number of people who suffered from mental stress. Yet, Chinatown's plight was underreported in the media and overlooked by public agencies and private organizations that provided relief funds.

The third reason is to celebrate the heroics of people such as Zhe (Zack) Zheng, who was last seen heading back into the World Trade Center to save lives after he had already safely exited; Officer Isaac Hoopii, who was among the first to arrive on the scene at the burning Pentagon, and saved a dozen lives; and Betty Ann Ong, the flight attendant, who first alerted ground authorities of the terrorists on American Airlines Flight 11 and calmly gave critical information to them for 20 minutes. Lastly, OCA wanted to capture stories on the impact of September 11 on certain APIAs and the chosen ways in which they responded.

Voices of Healing compiles stories of APIAs who experienced the immediate aftermath of the terrorist attacks or were indirectly affected. These APIAs organized and participated in candlelight vigils and media events, held fundraisers, and created artistic expressions to bring to public life their inner sentiments.

While by no means fully inclusive of all stories that exist, this publication is an opportunity for APIAs to find a voice for their experiences and to bring healing to the open wound that was inflicted on us all on Sept. 11, 2001. The individuals and organizations that were involved in *Voices of Healing* were moved by the people who were directly affected by the tragedy, particularly the victims' families. As we worked on the publication, we also found personal healing from their stories. As our readers browse through *Voices of Healing*, we hope they will feel the same.

1 49 Minutes of Terror....

CHAPTER 1
TERROR STRIKES

The North Tower of the World Trade Center is in flames after it was hit by American Airlines Flight 11.

Courtesy of Asian American Federation of New York

Smoke escapes into the clouds from the World Trade Center following the impact of the second hijacked plane.

A fiery explosion erupts from the World Trade Center following the impact of the second hijacked plane.

TERROR STRIKES

Timeline
149 Minutes of Terror

> 7:59 a.m.
American Airlines Flight 11 departs Boston, bound for Los Angeles with 81 passengers and 11 crewmembers.

> 8:14 a.m.
United Airlines Flight 175 departs Boston for Los Angeles with 56 passengers and 9 crewmembers.

> 8:20 a.m.
American Airlines Flight 77 departs Washington Dulles Airport for Los Angeles with 58 passengers and 6 crewmembers.

> 8:42 a.m.
United Airlines Flight 93 leaves Newark for San Francisco with 37 passengers and 7 crewmembers.

> 8:46 a.m.
American Airlines Flight 11 crashes into floors 94 through 98 of the North Tower of the World Trade Center.

> 9:03 a.m.
United Airlines Flight 175 crashes into floors 78 through 84 of the South Tower of the World Trade Center.

> 9:37 a.m.
American Airlines Flight 77 hits the Pentagon.

> 9:59 a.m.
The South Tower collapses.

> 10:03 a.m.
United Airlines Flight 93 crashes in Shanksville, Pennsylvania, 80 miles southeast of Pittsburgh.

> 10:10 a.m.
A portion of the Pentagon collapses.

> 10:28 a.m.
The North Tower collapses.

Courtesy of Asian American Federation of New York

The South Tower collapses while the North Tower is burning with black, oily smoke.

The Twin Towers are disintegrating into a fury of smoke.

Courtesy of Asian American Federation of New York

John Lee escapes from the collapse of
the South Tower.

*T*ERROR
STRIKES

Rescue workers survey damage to the World Trade Center,
and continue rescue operations in the burning wreckage on
Sept.11, 2001.

TERROR STRIKES

Firefighters spray water into the Pentagon to put out the fires after a hijacked plane crashed into the building. In the back view, the Washington monument stands tall.

A tank rolls into the streets of Manhattan.

Sunlight exposes the damage to the Pentagon.

Returning from Ground Zero, a Chinatown fire truck is covered with fallen debris and dust.

TERROR STRIKES

Courtesy of Rick Ho, *Sing Tao Newspaper*.

Survivors witness the terror nearby the fallen towers.

‹

Courtesy of Yujian Liu, *Coastside Magazine*

Mobs of people escape from the Twin Towers to the Brooklyn Bridge, which is covered with clouds of heavy dust.

⌃

19

A girl passes by a public space papered with flyers of the missing from the World Trade Center.

Immediately after the attacks on the World Trade Center, family and friends of missing persons plastered public walls with flyers displaying their photos in hopes of finding information about their loved ones' safety and location. Tragically, none of these persons were found alive.

Bystanders in Greenwich Village on Sept. 13, 2001 look at a van covered with posters of people missing from the World Trade Center disaster.

Courtesy of Local 23-25 UNITE

A bystander looks at the portraits of the missing
on a wall outside a hospital on 30th Street.

∧

On September 11, 343 firefighters....

CHAPTER 2
HEROES

Former President Bill Clinton visits with Port Authority police officer David Lim and his dog Sirius one year before the World Trade Center (WTC) attacks. Officer Lim was saving lives when he himself was trapped for five hours in the WTC rubble before being rescued. Sirius was the only dog to perish on Sept. 11, 2001.

Courtesy of David Lim

"I'm lucky to be alive. Everything around us was obliterated."

David Lim
Port Authority Police Officer
By Aryani Ong

On Sept. 11, 2001, New York City Port Authority police officer David Lim had just completed his morning rounds checking incoming trucks for explosives when he felt the building shake.

"My first thought was that there was a package that got by us," Lim said. The 23-year police veteran turned to his bomb-sniffing dog and partner, a Labrador named Sirius.

"I'm getting people out," Lim told Sirius. In the basement where his office and kennels were located, Lim decided that he would leave Sirius behind.

"I told Sirius I promised I would come back and get him. And that's the last time I saw him," Lim said. Sirius was the only dog that died in the World Trade Center.

Lim, 45, climbed to the 44th floor of the North Tower. He witnessed the second plane crash into the South Tower.

"I saw this debris and fire coming toward the window. It blew out the window and knocked me and everybody there down," he said. "When the second one hit, I knew we were in trouble and we were under attack."

The impact knocked him down to the ground. At that point, Lim rounded up the people on the floor and led them down the staircase.

"I told people, 'Keep on going down,'" he said. Meanwhile, the officer checked the floors to make sure that they were clear and looked for people who needed assistance.

On the fourth floor, he and another firefighter stopped to help a handicapped woman down the stairs when the building collapsed.

"You could hear the floors pancake. I'm lucky to be alive. Everything around us was obliterated," Lim said.

At the top of the rubble, Lim, firefighters, and a civilian were trapped for five hours. "We were waiting for the end," he said. The group was rescued, and none sustained major injuries.

But Lim had lost his best friend. Sirius's remains were found five months later. They were carried out with full honors, and a flag draped across the dog's bag.

Today, Lim has a new partner, Sprig. Nationally recognized due to the media spotlight, Lim has also been busy speaking at several public events. He recalls one engagement in particular that helped him deal with the past: " I've spoken to children at a Korean American summer camp, and their parents would later send me letters thanking me for speaking to them. I do not know if it takes the edge off, but it makes me understand why I survived."

"When I grew up, there were no Asian American and Pacific Islander role models," he said. "Now I've been called upon to fulfill a role, and I accept it. But my notoriety came at a great cost. "

Officer David Lim (L) watches Debbie Stonebraker unveil her portrait of his K9 partner Sirius, who was killed during the terrorist attack at the World Trade Center, during a memorial service at Liberty State Park on April 24, 2002, in Jersey City, New Jersey.

On September 11, 343 firefighters, 37 Port Authority police officers, and 23 police officers gave their lives in the line of duty. They were praised for their heroism, strength, and sense of duty.

"Come over here. Head toward my voice."

"I'm lucky to be alive. Everything around us was obliterated."

"When our guys got out of the area, all of us sat in a huddle crying like children."

"When Tower Two was collapsing, the firefighters moved aside to let the civilians pass before them."

"My message: to live life to the fullest and be thankful for every day."

"I appreciate life every day."

HEROES
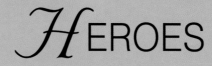

"Come over here. Head toward my voice."

Isaac Ho`opi`i
Pentagon Police Officer
By Aryani Ong

On a routine morning, Officer Isaac Ho`opi`i, 38, and his partner and dog, Vito, would be checking for bombs around the Pentagon. The team worked for the K-9 division of the Pentagon police. But on the morning of September 11, they were at the veterinarian's office. Then Ho`opi`i heard the radio call.

"Emergency. Emergency. Plane has hit the Pentagon."

Ho`opi`i felt an adrenaline rush. His home station had been hit. He sped the three-mile distance to the Pentagon, blowing out his car's transmission on the way. He and Vito arrived a minute and a half later. No firefighters had yet arrived on the scene.

Ho`opi`i saw flames licking out from the building, black smoke, and a huge hole cut into the western side of the Pentagon. The metal remnants of the downed airplane were strewn all over the ground. Immediately, Ho`opi`i noticed blown-out windows and people climbing out, coughing. Leaving Vito in the car, he ran to the building, bringing people to a grassy area where a triage was being set up.

From the building, Ho`opi`i heard voices calling out. Without the protection usually donned by a firefighter-mask, long-sleeved jacket, oxygen tank, Ho`opi`i found an open space in the wall and ran inside.

"There wasn't time to make a decision on what equipment you needed," Ho`opi`i said. "When you hear people screaming desperately for help, you know that a person's life is depending on every critical second. Time was an essence."

As the burly officer found people on the ground, he carried them over his shoulder and outside to safety. Then he would plunge back into the fiery fortress. By his own estimation, Ho`opi`i made 10 trips inside the burning building.

A couple of times, people warned him against entering the danger zone.

Courtesy of Isaac Ho`opi`i

Officer Isaac Ho`opi`i poses with his dog and partner, Vito. Ho`opi`i saved more than a dozen lives at the Pentagon. He carried out the wounded and guided people with his voice when they were lost in the smoke.

He chose to ignore the warnings. "We can't leave them," he thought, of the people whose voices he heard.

Fellow officers called to him to halt before Ho`opi`i initially entered the Pentagon. "Live wires," he was cautioned. He entered anyway. After his second or third trip outside carrying out survivors, firefighters who had arrived on the scene showed him a machine reading that proved the air was toxic. He skirted around the firefighters through a different entrance and ran back inside.

He battled the heat and pushed away the debris. But he could not see through the black smoke. He called out, "Is anyone in here?" In response, he heard cries. "Help me!"

"I said, 'Come over here. Head toward my voice,'" Ho`opi`i recalled. Using his voice, the officer guided a group of people who were within 50-75 feet of safety. Weeks later, Ho`opi`i would read in the newspaper about a survivor who described a guardian angel whose accented voice guided him outside.

"I felt so relieved that someone got out," the officer said. "After September 11, I would only remember that people were calling out for help and not knowing whether they got out." In all, Ho`opi`i carried or guided 17 people out of the building. Among them, three did not survive.

Immediately following September 11, heroism was the last thing on Ho`opi`i's mind. He had stayed at the Pentagon for 24-36 hours straight, only going home to shower and then return to work. For the next six months, he logged 16 hours a day, seven days a week.

"During the traumatic time, I had to stay focused. I was talking to my dog," Ho`opi`i said. "He loves you unconditionally. He just listens." But eventually, the strain of the long hours affected the team. "He was so overstressed, I had to retire him," Ho`opi`i said of his bomb-sniffing partner. Now, Vito lives at Ho`opi`i's home.

For his heroic feats, Ho`opi`i was awarded the Congressional Medal of Valor, the highest honor this country bestows upon a citizen. He carried the Olympic torch on its journey to the Salt Lake City Winter Games in 2002. He has been interviewed by national news media including CNN, the "Today Show," *The Washington Post*, and *U.S. News* and *World Report*. The governor of Hawaii named a day after the officer in his honor.

But this hero may have paid the ultimate price for his deeds. After September 11, he coughed up black mucous. His doctor warned him that he might have been exposed to asbestos. If he was, he has approximately 10 years to live.

For now, however, Ho`opi`i is focused on normal life activities. He coached his daughter's softball team. He is singing again on the weekends with a band called the Aloha Boys. A native Hawaiian (he also has Portuguese and Chinese lineage), he was trained by ear to perform traditional Hawaiian songs in kiho'alu, or slack key, on the guitar. The band performed at a benefit concert sponsored by Asians United to Raise Awareness (AURA) Fund to raise money for the victims of September 11.

Ho`opi`i said he was proud to represent Hawaii on the day that America was attacked. Aware that he is looked upon as a role model, he gives speeches at schools when he returns to Hawaii.

"I grew up on the island," Ho`opi`i said. "I tell the children, 'If I can make it, sitting in that same chair where you are, then you can make it.'"

Rebecca Canalija (left) visits Ground Zero with her colleague, Terry Jung (right), three days after the attacks.

"I appreciate life every day."

Rebecca Canalija
Emergency Nurse
By Icy Smith

Two years after September 11, Rebecca Canalija, a native of Zamboanga del Sur, Philippines, still carries the painful memories of victims' charred bodies, fragments of flesh, open fractures of the living, distorted extremities of the living and dead, and the agonizing moans. She has been diagnosed with post-traumatic stress disorder.

On September 11, Canalija, an emergency nurse, was working in the emergency room at New York University Downtown Hospital, just two blocks from Ground Zero. Twenty minutes after the first plane crashed into the World Trade Center's North Tower, wounded people began to be admitted to the hospital. Canalija learned about the terrorist attacks from the increasing number of victims brought from the scene of devastation. After the South Tower collapsed, she knew her day would not be easy. A cloud of dust and debris engulfed the hospital, and the lobby turned into a crowded room with ghostly images. The building lost its power and phone service. The hospital relied on a backup generator. Canalija remained calm, and continued her medical duties even without electricity.

Firefighters and emergency rescue workers were in shock, and cried in the lobby and emergency room. After they were treated for eye burns, chest pains, and other minor injuries, they went back to the destruction site.

Within the first two hours, about 350 patients came into the hospital. The lobby and cafeteria became extensions of the emergency room. There were critically injured patients with third-degree burns, head traumas, broken bones, and chest injuries caused by falling debris or being trampled in stairwells at the World Trade Center. "A woman in her late 20s came in with her hair totally burned off. Another victim was severely burned with a blackened, claw-like hand. Many suffered from smoke inhalation," said Canalija. "At one point, I was holding a man's cracked head in a stretcher, and his brain fell into my hands. I learned later he didn't make it."

For patients who had respiratory problems, Canalija intubated them for oxygen. She will not forget David Bernard, whose lungs had collapsed from a crush injury. Bernard asked her if he was going to die. Canalija took care of him for weeks. He died on Dec. 11, 2001, three months after the attacks. Later, Bernard's wife, Nancy, sent Canalija a letter, thanking her for the loving care she gave to Bernard. In Nancy's letter, she said she would never forget the Filipino American nurse who had become a part of Bernard's family.

At 10 p.m. on September 11, Canalija went to Ground Zero to deliver medical supplies. "I was devastated when I saw the mountain of rubble. Exhausted firefighters lay on the ground. I couldn't stop saying, 'Oh my God'," Canalija recalled.

She went home at 1:30 a.m. Her nine-year-old daughter, Sarah, was anxiously waiting for her. Canalija, a single mother, finally broke down and cried for hours. In the following weeks, she could not close her eyes without seeing the traumatic images and hearing the moaning. "Every time I talked about 9/11, I would be out of control and cry," Canalija said with emotion.

At the first anniversary memorial service, Canalija was one of those honored to read the names of the victims of the terrorist attacks. "It was very moving and difficult for me on that day. I cried and grieved for the heroic souls. I can never forget the horrific experience of September 11," Canalija recalled while choking back tears.

Canalija was a recipient of the "Frontline Heroes Recognition Award" given by the Philippine Independence Day Committee and the Philippine Consulate General in New York. She was among the "Faces of Ground Zero," an exhibit by award-winning LIFE magazine staff photographer Joe McNally. The tribute honored the heroic deeds of Canalija and other September 11 heroes. She was pictured in her white nurse's uniform. Her photograph was featured in the companion book *Faces of Ground Zero: Portraits of the Heroes of September 11, 2001.*

"I saw great deeds in this horrific act. People from the local community and all over the country gave their support and respect by sending us goodies and gifts. We received coffee beans from Hawaii, pizzas from California, and Chinese cuisine from the restaurants in New York's Chinatown every day. We didn't need to buy food for a month," Canalija said with laughter. "I appreciate life every day."

Sarah Canalija (right) proudly stands beside the seven-foot portrait of her mother, Rebecca, which is part of the traveling exhibit "Faces of Ground Zero."

Courtesy of Rebecca Canalija

27

Shin Cho (left) and Corporal J. Pichardo (right) pose at the New York City Marine Corps Ball in November 2001. Cho cleared several floors of people and assisted firefighters with carrying equipment up and down 14 floors. He particularly remembers a firefighter whom he met and later learned perished in the collapse.

Courtesy of Shin Cho

$\mathcal{H}$EROES

"When Tower Two was collapsing, the firefighters moved aside to let the civilians pass before them."

Shin Cho
Marine Reservist
By Todd Leong

I came to the United States from Seoul, Korea, in 1984, grew up in Queens, and have been in New York for 18 years. I consider myself to be a true-blooded New Yorker. I joined the Marine Corps Reserves in 1995. I wanted to give back to the country that had given me the opportunity to realize my potential.

On Sept. 11, 2001, I began my workday at the Bank of America around 6:30 a.m., as usual. We were located on the 81st floor of One World Trade Center. We had just moved up there from the 10th floor two months earlier.

Around 8:45 a.m., the first plane struck. There was a loud explosion; then the world around me began to crumble. I initially dove under my desk. At first I thought an earthquake was hitting New York, but I realized that I wasn't in San Francisco and it was highly unlikely in New York. I ran to the windows. It was raining paper and debris like a ticker-tape parade. Bodies were falling, but I couldn't believe my eyes. Down below, I saw the body of a woman that had landed on a rooftop. Everyone was in shock and disbelief. Nobody knew what had happened, but we knew it was bad.

We wanted to get out, but we knew not to take the elevators in a fire. How would we all walk down from the 81st floor in time? People started to panic. Some women and I began to cry. Senior managers started leading the evacuation. I directed people to the stairs. When they were gone, I ran around and cleared the floor to make sure there was no one left.

As I started to go downstairs, I ran into two other associates. We teamed up to clear alternating floors for people left behind. I was surprised to find people sitting at their desks still in shock. I helped them regain their senses to evacuate the building.

That day, I saw the best and worst of people. Some people were trampling others in their desperate attempts to escape. A part of me understood their actions; after all, they all just wanted to get out alive. Some people were old, and wanted to wait for the firemen to arrive because they were too tired. Some people were obese, and couldn't get down the stairs easily. Other people had difficulty breathing because they were asthmatic. So I helped them down the stairs. People were stone-faced. They were like shells of people. I guess that's what shock does to you. I had to scream and slap them to get them moving. I tried to pair older persons with younger ones, healthier ones with less healthy ones. Many people were willing to assist with the buddy system. I was running around like a madman pairing them.

The fire that had started after the initial impact was working its way down. Smoke began to fill the air. Electrical fires were starting here and there. Ceilings began to crumble, but no one at the time imagined the building would collapse.

At the time, I didn't think, "I have to save people." But instinctively, I was doing what I thought I had to do. I

didn't know if it's a brave thing, a smart thing, a heroic thing, but I just felt that I had to get people out. If people are about to get hurt, you protect them. That's what I was taught. That's how I was raised. That's all I was doing. I was running on instinct. I reacted as my Marine training had taught me, focusing on the task at hand and ignoring the chaos around me.

Around the 70th floor, I learned there were two middle-aged men trapped in the elevator. I tried to force the doors open but couldn't. I kept telling them I would get something to pry it open and they kept yelling at me to get away. The smoke was getting into the elevator and they couldn't breathe. "The firefighters are going to come rescue us," they said, all the while urging me to leave them. I moved on. Later, I heard some noise and destruction behind me. I didn't think the men made it out alive.

Around the 60th floor, as I was running around, I realized that most of the people had already cleared out. I started my own escape from the burning building.

Around the 30th floor, I ran into the first firefighter, huffing and puffing his way up. He was a heavy-set white man. I asked him if he was ok. He said, "Yeah, just get the hell out!" I told him, "Just give me the pack off your back and let's go up together." He looked at me funny for a second and then he gave me his gear; so I put his oxygen tank on my back. We started running up together. As we rested on the 44th floor, I told him about the two people stuck in the elevator. I also gave him a damage assessment and told him how far the fire had gotten in the building.

I descended again, and ran into more firefighters, who were all exhausted but still going. I helped them with their gear. I carried picks and axes, hoses, oxygen tanks, and medical kits for four or five floors. I don't even know how many times I ran up and down the stairs. I was pumping with adrenaline at the time. I don't know how I was able to run so much. By the 40th floor, some firefighters had to

HEROES

rest. They were just too tired. But a couple firefighters went farther up.

As I was helping the firefighters, I started a conversation with a firefighter named Manny. He was a good-looking Hispanic man in his early 30s. He had a great attitude about the whole situation. He was stoic yet had a smile on his face. He knew he had a mission at hand. Amidst the chaos, there we were, carrying on a normal conversation. "Give me your business card. I'll buy you a beer when this is all over," he said. I looked at him and said, "You know what? I'll buy you the beer. It looks like you're doing more work." From there, we parted ways.

Up to that point, none of us knew what had really happened in Tower One. I had heard people pass by and say that a plane hit the building. I thought a pilot had flown a small Cessna into the building by accident. We couldn't fathom that it was a planned terrorist attack.

Then, while I was evacuating the people, the second plane hit. I thought, "Wow, that's no accident. Something terrible is happening." For the first time, I felt fear. And I saw fear in the faces surrounding me. It finally hit me that I could actually die that day.

I started down the stairs again. When I reached the lower 30th or the upper 20th floors, again I found myself in the company of firemen. The building suddenly rocked and began to tremble. Tower Two was collapsing with a thunderous roar. We all jumped for cover, ducking. A firefighter covered me.

We started hearing over the radio, "Tower Two fell, Tower Two fell, Tower One is going, get the hell out!" Among the civilians, there was a mad rush down the stairs. There were still teams of firefighters on each floor. When Tower Two was collapsing, they moved aside to let the civilians pass before them. That was one of the many heroic deeds I saw that day.

As for myself, I thought, "I need to get the hell out." People were backed up on the eighth or ninth floor, but eventually everybody got out. I emerged from the exit facing the West Side Highway. September 11 began as a beautiful sunny day, but when I came out it was pitch black from all the debris and ash in the air.

I ran to Warren Street. I saw a parking lot and grabbed a phone in a booth and made a call to my mother to tell her I was ok. As I hung up, I heard rumbling and turned around. The scene was like something right out of a Godzilla movie. I saw everybody running. I saw a cloud of smoke and ash rushing toward me. I tried to run away, but within seconds we were all engulfed in the darkness. We couldn't see or breathe. The ash was everywhere. When the air finally began to clear up, I walked through Chinatown and over the Manhattan Bridge. As I walked over the bridge, I was a zombie. Everyone around me was just a shell of his or her former self. Their eyes were just huge, dilated, looking into nothing, and the people just walked. I walked directly onto the Brooklyn-Queens Expressway. I flagged down a vehicle. The driver happened to be Chinese American man who spoke very limited English. He drove me to Elmhurst, a few miles from my house. I hitched another ride from an Arab man to my parents' Laundromat in Jackson Heights. They were both very understanding of my situation and what had just happened.

I saw my mother. She was worried, but not hysterical. She knew I worked downtown but did not know that I actually worked inside the Trade Center Towers. My father realized that I had been through a traumatic experience. He had fought in the Vietnam War, and had seen death and destruction. He just said he understood if I didn't want to talk.

I took a shower, and then sat down to watch TV. I joined the rest of the world in disbelief and shock. How could anyone in their right mind fly two planes into the World Trade Center?

Then it hit me. I wondered if the firemen who had let me out ahead of them escaped. So I put on my Marine uniform and drove back. All the roads leading downtown had been blocked off, but I had my military ID and gained access. The governor had activated the National Guard, and I saw them arriving in droves. Anyone in a civil service uniform was rushing to Ground Zero.

Because the buildings were still burning, we were not permitted close to the site. I thought the fires would have been extinguished by then, but I could still feel the heat blocks away. So I stood there and waited for the go ahead to go inside.

After about an hour of waiting, we heard another rumble. Building Seven was collapsing. Everyone started to run. It was deja vu all over again. At that point, I had enough. I felt that I would end up getting emotional if I stayed. So I went home, took a shower, and went to sleep. That was the end of the September 11 for me.

I didn't believe in post-traumatic stress disorder. So I engulfed myself in work. Two weeks later, I was called into service by the Marine Reserves to augment the National Guard in protecting the city, as a member of the anti-terrorist task force. I kept even busier. I tried not to think about that day so that I would not bring myself down.

A month later, while I was on guard duty, I saw a poster with all the missing firefighters. I started looking at the pictures. Manny had a very distinctive face. I saw a picture of Manuel Delvalle. I thought, "Manuel? Manny? Damn!" Of the 300 or so Bank of America employees in the building that day, four people were lost. I had worked with them on a daily basis. I was affected by their deaths, but when I saw that Manny didn't make it out, it really struck home. I was down for a few days just reliving those few minutes in the stairs. I may have been the last person that he spoke to that day. I

watched him carry on with his duties until his dying moments.

Men don't cry. That's how I was raised. But that day I finally broke down and cried. That was when the stark reality of September 11 finally hit home.

Benny Hom stands in front of his fire
truck in Chinatown, New York.

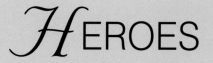

"When our guys got out of the area, all of us sat in a huddle crying like children."

Benny Hom
Firefighter
By Benny Hom

I was in a classroom attending a training at the Fire Academy on Randall's Island when we were told by our superior at the fire station, "Get on the school bus, a plane went into the World Trade Center." After reaching the Brooklyn Battery Tunnel, we teamed up in groups of two with walkie-talkies and ran toward the World Trade Center.

We were two blocks away when the second tower came down. It was instant darkness; dust everywhere. We ran behind a building for shelter and lay down on the ground. When we got up, we couldn't see well, but we could hear well. We got closer to the site. We came upon a car that was crushed by the falling debris. Four of us started digging and we saw an arm belonging to a man trapped in the debris. The man, a fellow fireman, was alive. We dug him out and radioed on the walkie-talkie, "We have Lieutenant Fuentes, but we don't know where we are." The fireboat radioed back. "Listen for a horn and head to the water."

We made it to the water. Things were really crazy. People were in shock, walking in circles. There was a firefighter walking around holding a leg. I told him to sit down, but he kept saying, "No, but I got a leg." We heard guys on the walkie-talkie saying, "Come get us" or "I'm hurt, please help me." Then nothing. When our guys got out of the area, all of us sat in a huddle crying like children.

Courtesy of Local 23-25 UNITE

A small shrine stands outside a firehouse in Chinatown, displaying letters and notes in Chinese. One firefighter remembers a horde of people who came to the firehouse with dumplings, fish, and Chinese cookies.

33

$\mathcal{H}$EROES

"My message: to live life to the fullest and be thankful for every day."

Richard Wong
Port Authority Police Officer
By Carolyn Troy

There are many heroes of September 11, that have made an imprint on America and will always be remembered for their heroism, bravery, and courage. Yet, there are still many amazing stories such as this one that have remained untold.

Richard Wong, a Port Authority police officer of 22 years, was on the scene following the second plane's descent into the South Tower of the World Trade Center. A second-generation Chinese American—born and raised in Chinatown, just blocks away from the World Trade Center—watched as history happened. Wong, 53, was working his regular 10 p.m. to 6 a.m. shift on Sunday night, Sept. 10, 2001, and was asked to work four hours of overtime. Around 5 a.m. he realized that he had a prior commitment. He returned to his apartment on Mulberry Street in Chinatown. Later, he was awakened by the first airplane smashing into the North Tower

Courtesy of Richard Wong

Port Authority police officer Richard Wong poses at the concourse level of World Trade Tower One. This photo was taken after Wong's police academy graduation ceremony, which was held on the 88th floor of World Trade Tower One in 1983.

34

of the World Trade Center complex. The shock of the collision shook his building. At first, he thought the noise had come from one of the courthouses across from him or one of the municipal offices across the street. But as he looked out his window, he saw black smoke coming from the World Trade Center. He threw some water over his face, and when he looked out the window again he saw the second plane hit the South Tower. He called his command center and was ordered to report to work.

Wong got dressed and made his way toward the Holland Tunnel, which was a scene of mass chaos and confusion. He saw decontamination stations, along with ambulances and fire trucks arriving from the neighboring townships in New Jersey. When he arrived at the tunnel, he was handed a set of keys and told to go to the World Trade Center with no more specific instructions.

Wong spent the remainder of his day and night shuttling injured people into patrol cars and dropping them off at the closest available hospitals. He brought the majority of injured people to St. Vincent's Hospital and New York University Downtown Hospital. Wong said he was basically shoving into cars people who appeared to be injured, many bleeding and moaning in agony.

Sadly, he later learned that he had lost 37 of his colleagues and comrades on that day, something he will never forget. He acknowledged that the tragedy would have been worse if people did not evacuate others in time. Fortunately, many lives were saved. Wong said, "I was very glad to see the response from neighboring towns and a lot of volunteers. It was very heartwarming. The city stuck together in that crisis. The people are a credit to the city."

The events of September 11 took an economic toll on all of New York City, especially the downtown area of Manhattan where streets were blocked off and tunnels and bridges were closed, restricting admittance in and out of the area. Only emergency personnel, doctors, and nurses were granted full access to Lower Manhattan. As for Chinatown, Wong described it as a ghost town, the streets empty for two weeks after the tragic event as businesses closed down of their own accord. A lot of businesses were forced to close permanently because they were unable to maintain rent. Workers were laid off. He said, "It was hard to distinguish what was out of business and what had just closed."

Chinatown thrives on tourism and Wong feels it is important for people to come back down to Chinatown and re-establish it as a major attraction on Lower Manhattan. Wong sees tour buses back again as a good sign, but feels things are getting back to normal too slowly. Wong said, "It was a shock to everybody whether you were Asian American or not, and of course a lot of people suffered a great loss, especially the Chinese American people because of the proximity to Chinatown. It was a landmark. People knew where Chinatown was and could always find it. For Asian Americans, it was a place to go to the concourse and shop. Looking out on the Plaza, it's not there anymore."

As a Port Authority police officer and a native to the Lower Manhattan area, he said, "I find it heartbreaking, because as a young man I went down on bicycle, walked, ran, and saw them construct the towers one by one and floor by floor, and to witness them coming down was just horrifying. The World Trade Center will hold a definite place in my heart."

Wong said, "I have a new lease on life. I could have been down there that day when the catastrophe stuck but somehow God wasn't ready for me yet and that is my message: to live life to the fullest and be thankful for every day."

The countless acts of bravery....

CHAPTER 3

SURVIVORS AND EYEWITNESSES

Courtesy of the Rafu Shimpo - Los Angeles News Publishing Company

Robert Ideishi poses with his wife, Susan, and their daughters, Erin and Jill, in his hometown of Los Angeles.

"The countless acts of bravery and genuine concern for fellow human beings are uplifting."

Robert Ideishi
Cost Accounting Manager
By Icy Smith

Around 8:20 a.m. on Sept. 11, 2001, Robert Ideishi, a cost accounting manager at Kingston Technologies, was attending an international trade seminar on the 55th floor of Tower One. He grabbed something to eat and took a seat in the back row of the classroom. Ideishi was sitting next to a door that led outside to the hallway. Through the door, he could see the outside of the building through a window in the hallway.

Soon, the instructor started the class and introduced himself to the seminar attendees. Then the attendees introduced themselves to one another. Suddenly, he heard a loud noise like a sonic boom. The building was shaking like crazy. It swayed to the left and to the right for seconds as if it was going to tip over into the Hudson River. Everyone froze. The instructor looked at Ideishi and asked him if it was an earthquake. "I don't know," Ideishi said.

Ideishi looked out the door and saw falling debris, flames, and smoke outside the window. One lady screamed, "We have to get the hell out of here!" Everyone got up and ran into the hallway. Ideishi tried to put his laptop and seminar notebook into his portfolio case. He was the last one to leave the room. About 25 people were running madly in the hallway. An African American man stood at one stairwell holding an open door and yelled, "Get in here now!" He forced everyone to get out. A mob of people ran into that stairwell, which was still lit and without smoke. Again, Ideishi was the last one to leave the floor. He let other people escape first without thinking he was in a real danger.

After he had descended two flights of stairs, he came to a complete stop. People screamed down the stairs, "What is going on?" In Ideishi's mind, there had been a bomb explosion above his floor. Stuck in the stairwell 50-plus floors above ground, he could only assume that the next blast would end it for him. He didn't think he had any chance to get out alive. No one's cellular phone was working. Everyone was frantic.

A man about a half flight of stairs above Ideishi started telling tales of the 1993 World Trade Center attack. He recalled many injured people and deaths. Women started to sob and moan. A woman wearing a blue pantsuit and white blouse said, "Would you please not tell your stories? You are upsetting everybody. We have to stay calm and get everybody out of here." The storytelling man shut up. Ideishi turned around and looked at the lady. He made eye contact with her. She winked at him.

"She made me laugh. She was right. I thought to myself, 'If she could stay calm, so could I,'" said Ideishi. But being calm didn't change Ideishi's thinking. He was really scared and distraught. The next 15 minutes were the saddest moments for him. Ideishi felt that he had no chance to survive. Tears started to well up in his eyes at the thought that he would never get a chance to say goodbye or see his wife, Susan, and his daughters, Erin and Jill.

When he reached the upper 40th floors, he heard, "Move to the right. Injured coming down!" One woman was badly burned and was being carried by civilians. Another woman had terrible black burn marks on her face and arms

and wore disheveled clothes. She was bleeding from her head, face, neck, shoulders, arms, and legs. Her eyes were glazed over as if she was catatonic. It was horrific.

Ideishi looked away and stared at the wall. A woman in her 30s in front of him was flabbergasted. She was staring, shaking, and crying, "Oh my God!" with her hand over her mouth.

Ideishi advised her not to look at the injured people. He gently put his hand on her shoulder and slowly turned her face to the wall. She continued to cry very loudly. One man, who appeared to be her business colleague came down two and a half flights to comfort her.

"It was amazing that everybody let him come down to be with her. At times, a few people would come down with injured people, claiming they knew the injured people. People were scared and tried to do what they could to save their lives," said Ideishi.

Someone shouted, "Blind man with a dog coming down!" Everyone stayed to the right against the wall. The blind man walked slowly down the stairs. "I saw many hands reach out and touch his right arm to make sure that he kept his balance," Ideishi recalled.

More women were crying. A heavy Latino woman had trouble breathing and sat on the steps in front of Ideishi, crying, "Just leave me here! I can't go anywhere. I can't make it." A thin, African American man in his late 60s reached down to touch her shoulders and said, "You have to keep going. You can't stay here." As if he had superhuman strength, he put his arms under her left arm and let her lean on him all the way down to the ground floor.

On the 40th floor, Ideishi saw the first group of firefighters. They were carrying heavy gear, hoses, picks, axes, shovels, and huge tanks. They were soaking wet from perspiration. A few of them collapsed to their hands and knees at Ideishi's feet.

Ideishi recalled that whenever one firefighter would collapse, another firefighter would take something off his fallen comrade's back to lighten the load. They would wait until the other exhausted firefighters were ready to go up again.

A fire chief explained that an airplane had hit the building. The way he described it, it sounded as though it was a little plane. He stopped Ideishi and asked, "What floor did you come from? Was there any damage? Did anyone get hurt? Were any windows blown out?"

After the fire chief assessed the situation, he said to everyone, "Don't worry! Try to stay calm and keep everyone else calm. We just came from downstairs. It's all clear. You guys

SURVIVORS & EYEWITNESSES

"The countless acts of bravery and genuine concern for fellow human beings are uplifting."

"I thought it was the end of the world."

"Dazed survivors dressed as gray ghosts gazed upward as human raindrops rained down."

"The day has left me with a deep sense of gratitude and love for all those who helped me and others."

"No amount of money can substitute for time."

"It was like D-Day with the atomic bomb. Dramatic and unforgettable."

"I realized that I had just experienced fear for the first time in my life."

"I had considered not going in to the office, but I didn't want to let the terrorists win."

"It was weeks before life at the Pentagon began returning to normal."

"I clenched my teeth to stop the tears that were welling up in my eyes."

are going to make it."

For the first time, Ideishi had hope. He really believed he was going to make it. Everyone was now calm. The reassuring words of the fire chief lifted the people's spirits. Ideishi passed crews of firefighters about every four to five floors. When he reached the fifth or sixth floor. He saw water, debris, and broken glass all over the floor. Everyone started to kick the glass out of the way toward the wall, clearing a safe path for the barefoot women who had taken their shoes off to walk down the stairs.

"It was pretty amazing. Everyone pitched in and helped in any way they could. I saw a couple of men lifting up and carrying a couple of women so they wouldn't have to walk at all," Ideishi recalled.

When he reached the first floor, the water was ankle deep. He saw a line of emergency workers, New York police, Port Authority police, FBI agents, and firefighters. They all bellowed out, "Move. Move. Don't look back!" Ideishi raced north of Tower One as he was instructed. There was falling debris and a cloud of dust. It had taken an hour and 15 minutes for him to escape.

Months after September 11, Ideishi still couldn't sleep through the night. He visualized the faces of the firefighters and policemen in his mind. They are his heroes. On the one-year anniversary of the Towers' collapse, he flew to New York from his hometown of Los Angeles to attend the memorial service at Ground Zero. He needed to pay his respects to the people who had saved his life on that fateful day. He felt it was his personal obligation.

"I saw so many terrible, horrific things. But the countless acts of bravery and genuine concern for fellow human beings that I witnessed are more uplifting. I can never forget the calm voices and the determined faces of the firefighters. It is extremely painful to think that they are all gone!" said Ideishi.

Courtesy of Steven Chen

After the September 11 tragedy, Steven Chen and his wife, Mary, felt that they were reborn. Here, Steven and Mary pose in China on vacation, September 2002.

"I thought it was the end of the world."

Steven Chen
Senior Software Engineer
By Icy Smith

Steven Chen was in his office on the 80th floor of Tower One on the morning of September 11. He was the Senior Software Engineer of Brut ECN. Chen started off his routine workday by getting a cup of coffee from the kitchen and checking his email. Around 8:46 a.m., the building shook for a few seconds. Chen was knocked out of his seat and pushed toward his computer monitor. He thought it was an earthquake. However, his co-worker saw the plane crashing into the building and screamed, "Our building was hit by a plane! We should get out of here!" A few women cried in panic. But most of them were calm and rushed immediately to the hallway.

Chen did not realize the danger. His office was only 14 floors below the point of impact. He organized his backpack, paperwork, books, and music CDs on his desk. Then he followed the other people who were descending the stairs to the 78th floor's Sky Lobby, which housed express elevators to the ground floor. At that time, most exit doorways were locked. Everyone was running around in a panic, looking for a stairwell that could lead to the ground floor. After 15 minutes, a building worker found a stairwell. The time was around 9 a.m. A flood of people ran down the stairs. Immediately, they formed two lines: one for women and seniors, and another for men and young people. Everyone seemed to follow unofficial rules and helped one another escape. People offered kindness. No one stopped to think about color or religion; everyone just helped everyone else.

At the 40th floor, Chen started seeing injured people with terrible burn marks on their bodies and clothes. "I saw deaths," one person said. But everyone remained calm. "We'll be there!" "We'll make it!" "Don't worry. Calm down!"

On the 18th floor, Chen saw the first stream of firefighters and police. "Move to the right! Move to the right!" people shouted. "It was hard to forget the bravery of firefighters carrying up the gear, hoses, and tanks. They embarked on a mission that was unimaginable," Chen remembers.

Chen managed to reach the lobby in an hour and a half. The floor was flooded. People were screaming. The situation became chaotic. He saw a line of firefighters, police officers, and reporters. "Don't stay here! Move! Keep moving!" an FBI agent yelled.

When Chen got out of Tower One, he realized that Tower Two had collapsed. He was traumatized. He began to run. He had only been running for two minutes when Tower One started to collapse. He heard a loud boom and saw a mass of dust and debris twisting around him. "Get the hell out of here!" people screamed.

"A 40-floor-high cloud of black smoke and dust scattered all over the place. There were all kinds of horrifying noises. I thought it was the end of the world," Chen recalled. Thousands were injured from the fallen debris. It was a miracle that Chen escaped unscathed.

"Dazed survivors dressed as gray ghosts gazed upward as human raindrops rained down."

Ankuresh Ghosh
Project Manager
By Abhijit Ghosh

Courtesy of Abhijit Ghosh

Through a detailed timeline, Abhijit Ghosh (left) relates the story of his father, Ankuresh Ghosh (right) who escaped from the World Trade Center.

SURVIVORS & EYEWITNESSES

Like several others, my family was personally affected by the events of September 11. My father, Ankuresh Ghosh, whom I called Baba, used to work on the 72nd floor of the World Trade Tower One. He survived. This is his story.

8:10 a.m.
That Tuesday morning began like any other workday. I took my jacket with my briefcase. As I stepped through the revolving door to enter the North Tower of the World Trade Center, I decided to walk through the Plaza. I always enjoyed seeing the stores and eating there.

On the 72nd floor, I greeted two co-workers, Bill and Ashish. I was asked to join them and Prem, another co-worker, for our daily coffee. I declined, due to my busy schedule.

8:40 a.m.
Papers were strewn across my desk as I settled in. I began to check my voice mail. A roar exploded above me. The building shifted 10 inches as I held onto my desk. Books fell as the building swayed back and then stood still.

Someone shouted, "What happened?"

Nobody answered. There was something wrong, though no alarms were ringing. It was just too quiet. I hurried to the elevator, but nobody was there. Then I walked into the lighted stairway. I saw about 20 people, including Bill and Ashish, walking down the stairs.

8:53 a.m.
I thought it was an accident. But I was not worried. The building was solid. I was sure that I would return to my 15-year-old briefcase and jacket. We created two single-line files. Everyone was calm.

I walked down about 10 flights. There were now more than 60 people walking down with us when I heard a voice from above.

"Make room. Move to the right. Someone hurt coming down."

I braced myself against the wall. I saw a white woman being carried by two people. She had burns all over her body.

9:01 a.m.
At the 56th floor, I saw the first crew of firefighters. They carried heavy oxygen tanks on their shoulders.

"Make one file to the right. Walk slowly and remain calm!"

I continued to walk down, reaching the 45th floor after about 15 minutes. Now everything was changing. I started to cough. Nobody was talking much. Smoke was now visible. Some people wrapped handkerchiefs around their mouths. And then I heard this second roar. The building shook but did not shift. Cries of concern broke out around me.

"Was that an explosion in our building?"
"A second plane crashed into the other tower."
"How do you know?"
"I got the news on my PDA."
"Dear God, help us!"

Panic settled in, and it grew. The hallway was crowded. Smoke wrapped around the stairway. That was when I had two thoughts. The first was that this was the act of a terrorist. The second was that I might not get out alive.

9:15 a.m.
Meanwhile, son Abhijit was in a Maryland office surfing the Web for New York paper reports on the Giants when he read the headlines. He called his mother.

"Ma, what floor does Baba work on?"

9:17 a.m.
As the Ghosh family struggled to understand the situation, Ankuresh Ghosh reached the 44th floor. Someone broke open the vending machine. A firefighter distributed water and soda to the people coming down. We were moving much slower now. At about the 34th floor, we saw the first emergency worker.

"You cannot go down this way. Go to the staircase across the lobby. One at a time."

His voice was steady and reassuring, which helped calm everybody. We entered into a darkened lobby. People formed a chain of support in the pitch-black hallway. Someone turned on a flashlight, cutting through the smoke. I could not see where Ashish or Bill was. Slowly, we walked through the lobby and went to the next staircase.

The first thing I noticed was water falling down from a broken pipe. It rained down the stairways, rising up to my ankles. My nostrils flared. I smelled that gas. I thought about myself, not God. I didn't think I was going to see my family again. I wanted to escape.

9:45 a.m.
On the second floor, we stopped moving, as the exit was blocked. The water was rising with the choking smoke. We returned to the third floor. The doors were propped open, and I reentered the Plaza. I could not believe what I was seeing.

Normally the Plaza is filled with exhibitors flying flags from different countries. Now, the floor was littered with glass and plaster. Explosions roared above me as glass continued to fall around me. There were not many people with me at this time.

10 a.m.

I threw my hands over my eyes as I walked out into the blinding daylight. I looked up in shock. The buildings were engulfed in black flames from the 45th floor upward. Trapped workers screamed for help. Fallen debris surrounded me, torn from the crashed airliners. Dazed survivors dressed as gray ghosts gazed upward, as human raindrops rained down.

I tried to find a working phone when a high-pitched scream whipped through the area. A wall of black smoke lumbered toward me. I ran as fast as I could for 10 blocks.

10:10 a.m.

I finally stopped running when I reached Canal Street. Traffic was choked. Radios were turned on. People, some shaking their heads, stood together listening to the radio.

"The Pentagon has been hit."
"There is one more plane unaccounted for."
"The terrorists hit at the same time!"

Thirty minutes later, I found an open bank with working phones.

"Hello?"
"It's me. I got out ok."
"Why did you call so late?" my wife cried. "I was worried!"

8:30 p.m.

Back home, I watched the news coverage. I turned to my wife.

"I don't think Prem made it out. He called his wife from the 82nd floor in the conference room and was fine. There was too much smoke outside. That was the last they talked."

One Year Later

All I feel is emptiness. The World Trade Center has been my home for 16 years. Life will not be the same anymore. We will survive with God's help.

42

Yoshiko Shoji, covered with gray soot, is reunited with her fiance, Larry Reeves.

"The day has left me with a deep sense of gratitude and love for all those who helped me and others."

Yoshiko Shoji
Credit Analyst
By Elizabeth R. OuYang

Yoshiko Shoji had just celebrated her birthday on Sept. 10, 2001. Little did she know that the bag and scarf she received as gifts would save her life the next day.

Working as a credit analyst on the 80th floor of the North Tower, she walked into her office just 15 seconds before the first plane hit her building. As she reached the 50th floor, her fiance called on her cellular phone. All she remembers from the conversation was that he told her he loved her.

At the 23rd floor, an army of sweating firefighters told them not to look in the courtyard and to take the stairwell instead of the escalator to the basement. Yoshiko looked anyway and saw burnt body parts scattered everywhere. Suddenly the building began to rumble and the sprinklers in the mall were activated. As the South Tower collapsed, a gust of dusty wind and glass burst into the mall connecting the two towers. Trapped in the mall, Yoshiko remembers falling down, grabbing her new scarf from her birthday bag, and wrapping it around her face to protect her from the dust. Suddenly she heard a rescue worker shouting to follow him, as he helped a 65-year-old Taiwanese American co-worker who had injured her leg in the fall. They made it out of the building and were two blocks away when the North Tower came crashing down. Totally shaken and in a daze, Yoshiko managed to walk to 36th Street, where she took a ferry to her fiance's home in New Jersey. On the ferry, she noticed her new bag had holes and slashes in it. She realized then it had saved her from the flying glass in the mall.

"The day has left me with a deep sense of gratitude and love for all those who helped me and others," she said. Impacted by the courageous volunteerism of others, Yoshiko is now volunteering to help the elderly deal with an array of social problems. "9/11 instilled in me an awareness of what is truly terrible and what is merely an inconvenience or a minor problem. I know that whatever challenges I face in the future, I will be able to think back and remember I made it through that day, so I can surely make it through this one, whatever it holds," said Yoshiko. "No matter where you are, you could be the victim of terrorism and everyone must cooperate to get rid of it."

43

SURVIVORS & EYEWITNESSES

"No amount of money can substitute for time."

J. Lau
Accountant
By J. Lau

On the day of September 11, I went to work early, arriving at 7:30 a.m. at Two World Trade Center, 63rd floor, because I had to meet a deadline. At 8:45 a.m., the time the first plane hit One World Trade Center, I was initially oblivious to it because my office faced the Hudson River. There was a loud bang like the sound of a metal cabinet falling to the ground and suddenly we could see through the windows streams of paper in the air. Then we smelled something burning. My co-workers and I immediately packed into an elevator to the sky lobby and then took the stairs down from the 44th floor. At the 36th floor, a guard told everyone to go back to work. He said World Trade Tower Two was fine. But I was feeling dizzy so I continued down to the lobby. I went outside and there were fireballs in the street. Crossing the street, I looked back and saw a "missile" striking Two World Trade Center and suddenly a fireball headed my way. Screaming, I fell to the ground for protection. I ran to my home in Chinatown. I've never been the same since.

I was raised to live for the future, the golden years. The events of September 11 made me realize the golden years, let alone tomorrow, may not come. I used to work so hard, declining many social events and dinners with family and friends. I have since realized that no amount of money can substitute for time. I've left my job and I am soul-searching for a job that will make me happy now, in the present time.

Yujian Liu is covered with dust and falling debris on the Brooklyn Bridge on Sept. 11, 2001.

"It was like D-Day with the atomic bomb. Dramatic and unforgettable."

Yujian Liu
Reporter
By Icy Smith

The phone rang. Yujian Liu, a reporter for *Coastide Magazine*, answered it. "Have you watched the news on TV?" Liu turned on his television. He saw Tower One burning under a cloud of black smoke. Immediately, he jumped up from his bed. He quickly changed his clothes and ran out of his home without washing his face or brushing his teeth. His first instinct was to rush to the disaster site and take photos to document the horror of the event.

Liu took the subway from Brooklyn to downtown Manhattan. On the train, someone said aloud, "Whoever did this must pay for this." Liu got off the train at Canal Street Station. He rushed to his office, intending to take his digital camera. He saw his secretary, Mary Chen, crying. Chen told him that her husband, Steven, was working on the 80th floor of Tower One. She tried to phone her husband several times. But no one answered, and she kept reaching his voice mail. Liu reassured her that Steven would come home safely. He grabbed his camera and left.

Liu took the subway to City Hall, one block from the World Trade Center. When he approached the catastrophic site, he saw a crowd of spectators watching in disbelief as the Twin Towers burned. Thick, black smoke and flames emanated from the top floors of the buildings. All surrounding businesses were closed. Suddenly, he heard a huge explosion and a loud rumble. The sound was horrifying. He saw the inconceivable image of the collapsing South Tower. A mountain of dust, rubble, and debris chased after people on the street. The scene was unbelievable, more like a Hollywood production. Debris was falling on him in a deluge. Mobs of dust-covered people started to dodge pieces as they fell.

"It was the first time in my whole life I have witnessed such devastation. It was dramatic and unforgettable," said Liu.

As a journalist and photographer, Liu started taking photos, capturing the helpless and horrified expressions of the onlookers witnessing the calamity. Later, he went back to the Federal Building Plaza on 26th Street. He saw many people covered with soot and ash starting to wash their faces in a fountain. Media crew members and FBI agents were among the crowd. An FBI agent stopped Liu from taking photos. Liu walked to the Brooklyn Bridge. At that time, bridges and tunnels were closed.

At 10:27 a.m., Liu witnessed the collapse of Tower One. There was a mountain of fiberglass in the air and a huge wave of thick dust. People raced to the Brooklyn Bridge, covering their mouths with their hands or shirts. "It was like D-Day with the atomic bomb. I worried about the toxins in the air. And I thought Steven must have lost his life in the fallen tower. I didn't have the courage to go back to my office and see Mary," said Liu.

While still in deep shock, Liu continued his mission to capture images of the destruction on the street and the devastated emotions of the people. Later, he rushed back to Ground Zero. He experienced difficulty breathing from inhaling layers of dust and possibly asbestos. Liu was seen by a police officer, and was eventually sent home from the site.

Later he learned that Steven had managed to escape. Weeks after September 11, Liu still had nightmares about his traumatic experience.

SURVIVORS & EYEWITNESSES

Reporter Ken Moritsugu was walking in the shadow of the World Trade Center during the attacks. He reported on the tragedy in the days following. Here, he is conducting an interview in Afghanistan.

Courtesy of Jim Barcus, *Kansas City Star*, KRT

"I realized that I had just experienced fear for the first time in my life."

Ken Moritsugu
Reporter
By Ken Moritsugu

It was the last day of a three-day conference at the World Trade Center Marriott. I was staying at a Best Western near South Street Seaport, about a dozen blocks from the Twin Towers. I went down to the buffet breakfast room and saw a report on the big-screen television that a plane had hit one of the towers. A witness talking to CNN on the phone described it as a big plane, I thought she said a 737. No way, I thought. Must be someone overexcited. It dawned on me that maybe I could see this from outside my hotel. I wandered outside, Styrofoam cereal bowl in hand, and sure enough, a small crowd was standing on the cobblestone street, watching the smoke trail up from one of the towers. Everyone was quiet, no one quite sure what was happening. Suddenly, the second tower exploded and a huge orange fireball burst out of its side. It was the second plane, but we didn't know it at the time because we couldn't see it from our vantage point. Could the fire have jumped from one tower to the other? The news was blaring from the cranked-up radio of a parked car. Someone heard several planes had been hijacked. "This is war," a man muttered angrily.

I went back to my hotel room to call my office in Washington, D.C. "Stay put," the early morning editor told me. "We may want you to stay and cover this story." I went down to the front desk to try to extend my reservation, but was told the hotel was all booked up. The clerk put me on a waiting list in case there were any cancellations. I packed my bags, left them with the front desk, and checked out. I patted my blazer pockets to make sure I had a notebook, pens, and a tape recorder. Then I headed toward the scene.

I walked briskly up Fulton Street, scribbling notes about the people lining the sidewalks. They stared up at the smoking Trade Center towers and chattered nervously on their cell phones. Fulton was one of those narrow, Lower Manhattan streets, and only the top halves of the towers were visible. Subway riders coming up from the station were just discovering what had happened. Some joined the crowd on the street; others took a look and continued on their way to work.

I was about four blocks from the site when one of the towers began to shimmy and then started dropping to the ground. Mass panic went on all around me. Everyone started sprinting as fast as they could away from the towers. Women shed their heels. "Is the tower going to fall on us? Is it going to knock over the buildings around us?" I looked over my shoulder and a 10-story-high wall of dust and debris was hurtling down the street toward us, funneled between the buildings that lined the narrow street. I turned down a side street, thinking the debris wouldn't turn. It didn't. It dissipated.

Ash hung in the air and settled on cars and other surfaces like a dusting of snow. A woman overcome by emotion sobbed; a stranger tried to comfort her. When I caught my breath, I realized that I had just experienced fear for the first time in my life.

I headed back to the hotel and start interviewing people who had gathered in the small lobby. One man was completely covered in gray ash. He wouldn't talk to me. I walked over to a nearby hospital to see if any victims were coming in. I met a Wall Street trader who was too close to outrun the debris cloud. He hit the ground behind a dumpster. All went black. Seconds elapsed. Still black. He wondered if he would suffocate and die. Slowly the cloud lifted. When I saw him he was outside the emergency room, chest X-rays in hand, taken to ensure he hadn't inhaled anything noxious.

Later that day, another surreal scene. An endless stream of people, workers, executives, students, all refugees, walked north under an elevated highway, trying to get home. Some walked across one of the great bridge spans over the East River to Brooklyn. Others headed farther north, uptown.

Back in the hotel lobby, I squeezed into a corner near an outlet and hurriedly bashed out a story on my laptop. No modem connection, so I dictated it over a phone to one of my editors. Then I headed out again. I found a staging site for emergency workers about six blocks from where the Twin Towers stood. I was taking in the scene when all of a sudden people start yelling and scrambling away. A 47-story building named Seven World Trade Center was collapsing. Yet again, I was running as if my life depended on it, this time with police officers, firefighters, ambulance drivers, and medics. We escaped with nothing more than another heavy dusting.

The sun was setting, and the collapse of Seven World Trade Center had knocked out both power and phone service in much of Lower Manhattan. The building had housed two electricity substations and its debris smashed a major phone line switching center nearby. A utility worker suggested it would be at least a week before power was restored.

Rooms were available at the Best Western. The front desk loaned me a flashlight to climb the stairs in the dark. But both my laptop and cell phone were running out of juice. I retrieved my bags and headed uptown to spend the night.

Ken Moritsugu, Economics Correspondent for Knight Ridder Newspapers, remained in New York City for 10 more days to cover the aftermath of September 11. He returned to New York in October to cover the anthrax death of Kathy Nguyen, went to London in December for a story on Richard Reid, who tried to blow up a plane with explosives in his sneakers, and reported on the U.S. military engagement in Afghanistan and Pakistan in May 2002.

SURVIVORS & EYEWITNESSES

Raghav Kotval reminisces about September 11: the day he evacuated the Pentagon and made his way through Washington, D.C., gridlock to get home. He had moved to the Pentagon only a month earlier to work as an attorney.

"It was weeks before life at the Pentagon began returning to normal."

Raghav Kotval
Naval Officer
By Raghav Kotval

I had been at the Pentagon for a little more than one month before September 11, having just moved to Washington, D.C., from Okinawa, Japan. That morning, my colleagues and I were informed through phone calls that a plane had hit the World Trade Center. Initially, I thought that it was merely an accident. But when we turned on CNN, we witnessed the second plane hitting the second tower. Not more than 10 minutes later, we heard an explosion and felt a blast. Located on an adjacent side of the Pentagon from the point of impact, we were not in any immediate danger.

Within seconds, however, I saw thick, black smoke billowing out of the building. We descended five levels from the top floor in an orderly fashion. Once outside, we were more shocked and more confused than scared. Not familiar with the smell of burning jet fuel, I feared the worst: that a bomb with chemical weaponry had been unleashed.

The members of my command were sent home. The metro system's inoperability required me to take the bus. Clogged streets slowed traffic, and the bus barely moved. On the bus, rumors ran amuck about what had happened. Frustrated by both the bus' slow movement and the rumors, I got off and started walking. Hours later, I finally got home to my basement apartment in Capitol Hill where I lived alone. Just delivered two days earlier, my worldly possessions were strewn all over the floor. I felt nothing.

I realized my parents would be concerned, so I tried to call them. It took 20 or 30 calls before I got through. My filial obligations fulfilled, I went out in search of food. Having had only an early breakfast, I did not realize how hungry I was until after I got home. The restaurants and neighborhood grocery store were open, as if it was business as usual. That evening I received no phone calls, and made none. I did not want to talk to anyone. I learned several weeks later that friends had tried to call me for days but were unable to get through.

On Sept. 12, 2001, I reported for duty. Already overwhelmed by the constant media attention to the attack, I dreaded entering the building again. The roof was still smoldering. Smoke was still in the air. A fine layer of soot covered everything; the hallways were black. Everything smelled of charcoal. However, the Pentagon was still largely functional. In the days to follow, we would see the bodies removed from the rubble laid out in the courtyard in the center of the building. It was weeks before life at the Pentagon began returning to normal.

Courtesy of Violeta Chen

Rashmi Agarwal, home sick from work, was jolted out of her bed when a plane crashed into the Pentagon. Here Agarwal stands on the roof of her apartment building, where she watches the smoke emanate from the Pentagon, in view in the background.

"I had considered not going in to the office, but I didn't want to let the terrorists win."

Rashmi Agarwal
Analyst
By Rashmi Agarwal

On the morning of September 11, I had gotten up to go to work, but I had a cold, so I went back to bed. I live in Arlington, Virginia, only two miles away from the Pentagon. Lying in bed, I heard a loud boom. The apartment building shook. At first, I didn't think anything of it. It never occurred to me that a plane would crash into the Pentagon. But when I got up and turned on the TV, I saw that the World Trade Center had been hit, and then the Pentagon.

I freaked out. I thought, "What am I going to do?" Outside, some people were walking; others were running in the street. The highways were closed, and the Metro subway system shut down. It was mayhem. I did not want to go outside. I knew another hijacked plane was still in the air, perhaps targeting the White House. I decided to stay in my apartment.

After a couple of hours, my roommate returned home from work. We went up to the rooftop. We could see fire trucks and police cars around the Pentagon. We could smell the smoke and see the huge, red-hot fire. It was so thick; it was scary. The smoke lasted until evening. I felt a mixture of anger, fear, and sadness. "Who could have done this, and why?" Even though I lived so close,

I could not bring myself to go the Pentagon after that day, although later I did pass by it on the highway. What I saw was that a large chunk of the Pentagon had been blackened and destroyed.

On Sept. 12, 2001, the federal government was open, so I went to work. I walked hurriedly to the Metro station. I was fearful. I had quickly learned not to take my safety for granted. I had considered not going in to the office, but I didn't want to let the terrorists win. I even had considered leaving Washington, D.C., now that it was a target. But I had lived and worked here for four years, and planted roots. I decided that I should not move just because terrorists might attack again.

September 11 affected me as an American. So it was ironic that on July 4, when my family usually holds a reunion at the Smithsonian Mall to watch the fireworks, my male family members balked. They knew they would get searched because they looked like the terrorists. We are South Asian Americans. We debated, but then we decided to go. And my male cousin was searched. I was not. I want security, but I would like to see security measures applied across the board.

SURVIVORS & EYEWITNESSES

Courtesy of Hyungwon Kang

Mark Keam, chief counsel to U.S. Senator Dick Durbin on the Senate Judiciary Committee, watched events unfold on TV from Capitol Hill. In the weeks to follow, he, along with several Hill staffers, would have to evacuate office buildings several times due to anthrax-tainted mail addressed to members of Congress.

"I clenched my teeth to stop the tears that were welling up in my eyes."

Mark L. Keam
Chief Counsel to U.S. Senator Dick Durbin
By Mark L. Keam

On Sept. 10, 2001, I was assisting the lead counsel on the hearing to review the prepared testimonies of witnesses who would come to Washington later that week to urge the senators to pass legislation that would allow undocumented high school students to continue on to college, notwithstanding their legal status. One of the witnesses scheduled to appear was a gifted high school girl from Chicago who, as far as I knew, would have made history as the first Korean American student ever to testify in Congress. I was excited about this historic possibility, and spent the day sharing this development with leaders of the Asian American and Pacific Islander community. I looked forward to a meaningful, but otherwise typical, week in the Senate.

So on the morning of September 11, when I drove to work, my mind was preoccupied with the details of what else had to be done for this hearing. Around 8:45 a.m., as I began crossing the 14th Street Bridge from Virginia into the District, I heard a breaking news report on WTOP AM news radio about an airplane that crashed into the World Trade Center in New York City. Both the reporter and I dismissed this very first report as just another terrible

accident, and assumed it must have been one of those small, private aircrafts that somehow got lost. But as I pulled into the parking lot just before 9 a.m., this news began to repeat again and again with more details trickling in.

One of the nice things about working in Congress is the ubiquitous presence of television sets in every office. Thus, as soon as I got to my desk a few minutes later, I saw that every TV network and cable news station was following this fast-breaking story. It was soon evident from the live camera feeds that the plane crash I had heard about on my drive in was not a small, private aircraft as I had imagined. By this time, the stations all confirmed that it was a commercial jet that crashed into the North Tower of the World Trade Center. My heart sank, and I remained glued to the TV on my desk.

Then, a few minutes after 9 a.m., I saw the live broadcast of another commercial jet crashing into the South Tower, followed by the audible gasp of all my co-workers who, like me, were frozen in our motions. We couldn't believe what we had just witnessed. We didn't know whether to leave our office or stay and work as if nothing had happened.

I called my wife, who was working from home that day. I told her to turn on the TV, which she had already been following that morning. She told me to come home immediately. I said, let's wait and see what this is all about. I sensed fear in her voice, so I wanted to sound as calm as possible. All the while, my heart was pounding 100 miles per hour.

Rumors began circulating. There was speculation of a wide-scale terrorist or military attack. There was rumor that Washington was another target, and that the Capitol would be next. I could hear people in my building already scrambling to leave.

At about 9:45 a.m., we received a call from Senator Durbin's secretary conveying the Senator's personal orders for the staff to leave the building immediately. At about the same time, the television screens flashed the latest news. "The Pentagon has been hit!"

I grabbed what personal belongings I could and rushed out with my co-workers. The halls of Congress where lobbyists and staff usually huddle now looked more like a Metro station during rush hour.

Once outside the Dirksen Senate building, I looked for other Durbin staff but didn't spot many of them. I finally saw our chief of staff, who told us to just go home and wait for further news about work. I made my way over to the parking lot but couldn't get my car out through the bottleneck, as every staffer was trying to do the same. Even after finally leaving the Senate parking lot, traffic was at a standstill.

Sitting in the traffic that hadn't moved in 20 minutes, I had one ear to the news on the radio and the other to my cell phone trying to call home. The news came in fuzzy and the wireless phone networks were overloaded. Every other minute, there was misinformation reported.

After trying to break through the busy signals for at least an hour, I finally got in touch with my wife and also with my mother in California to let them know I was ok. It took another hour of bumper-to-bumper crawl to eventually get home. I lived only eight miles from work, but because the bridge I would normally take to go home passes immediately next to the Pentagon, the authorities shut it down after the attack. I therefore had to cross the Potomac near Georgetown and drove a long way around through the Arlington suburbs before finally getting home to my wife, who was then eight-month pregnant with our first child.

The rest of the day was spent in front of the TV and on the phone with family and friends in New York, D.C., and across the country. By late afternoon, I heard reassuring words from President Bush and saw the leadership of our Congress gather on the Capitol steps to stand tall and strong in the face of the most devastating attacks we have faced on our soil. We heard them sing an impromptu "God Bless America," the words of which had never meant so much before that day.

The next morning, I drove by the Pentagon on the way to work. I could see the damage clearly, and was able to smell the horrible stench of smoke in the air, even from inside my car. I clenched my teeth to stop the tears that were welling up in my eyes. I had shed enough tears the day before, and I didn't want to show up to work with eyes any more red than they already were from lack of sleep.

Our world certainly changed on Tuesday, Sept. 11, 2001. That day impacted my professional and personal life in numerous ways. While I was not victimized in a direct way, I felt that the terrorists also attacked the very spirit of the work we do everyday as Congressional staff, which is to develop and uphold the rule of law in a free and open democracy. I have since recommitted myself to the serious responsibilities I take on every day as a lawyer, a public servant, and an American.

Many Asian Americans and Pacific Islanders....

Courtesy of the Ong Family

CHAPTER 4
VICTIMS

Betty Ann Ong was a flight attendant on American Airlines Flight 11, the first plane hijacked on Sept. 11, 2001. During a 23-minute phone call to ground authorities, she relayed vital information about the hijackers and the situation aboard the plane.

Betty Ann Ong
Courageous and Attentive Flight Attendant

The following is a tribute by the Ong Family to Betty Ann Ong. Betty Ann Ong was a flight attendant on American Airlines Flight 11 who heroically gave her life on the day America was attacked on Sept. 11, 2001.

Betty Ann Ong was born on Feb. 5, 1956, in San Francisco, California, to Mr. and Mrs. Harry Ong, Sr. She was the youngest of four siblings, a loving daughter, sister, aunt, and friend. She was warm, caring, thoughtful, and considerate, always thinking of others before herself. Gifted with a sense of humor, Betty had a knack for making people feel comfortable and putting them at ease. She had a smile that could light up a room and lift up a spirit. She could feed laughter to anyone's heart.

Betty's formative years were spent in San Francisco's Chinatown neighborhood. She drew strength from both her family and the Chinese American community and she embraced her cultural heritage with the utmost pride. She attended Jean Parker Elementary School. In 1969, Betty entered Francisco Middle School and graduated from George Washington High School in 1974.

Betty had a great love for children and senior citizens. She paid special attention to them whenever they were aboard a flight she was working. On many occasions, Betty would drive a half hour into Boston from her home in Andover, Massachusetts, to have lunch and take walks with senior citizens. To keep her legacy alive, the Ong Family has formed the Betty Ann Ong Foundation for children and senior citizens. The Betty Ann Ong Foundation will provide education scholarships as well as support activity centers for children and senior citizens.

Betty worked as a flight attendant with American Airlines for 13 years. She eventually rose to the position of purser, a head flight attendant. Betty was a tireless worker. Whenever she worked a late night flight, she would never sit down and relax. She would walk down the aisles and talk softly to the passengers who were awake and provide blankets to those who were asleep.

On Sept. 11, 2001, shortly after the takeoff of American Airlines Flight 11 at approximately 8 a.m. from Logan Airport in Boston, the plane bound for Los Angeles, California, was hijacked by five Middle Eastern men. It was the first plane of four to be hijacked that morning. Betty worked on Flight 11 as the number three flight attendant that morning. During the hijacking, Betty placed a call to American Airlines reservation agents in Raleigh-Durham, North Carolina, and relayed vital information about the identities of the hijackers and the hijacking situation on board the plane. She reported the situation: Two flight attendants were stabbed, one passenger was killed, and there was gas in the air that made breathing difficult in the first and business class areas of the plane. Betty's call was the first contact and the first indication that America was under attack, and her call eventually led to the shutdown of all flights nationwide to keep other possible hijackings from occurring. Under extreme duress and horrific circumstances we cannot imagine, Betty remained calm and professional during her 23-minute telephone call. Prior to the crash of the plane into the North World Trade Center in Manhattan, New York, Betty selflessly asked the ground crew to "pray for us," not just for herself. The Ong Family has had the opportunity to listen to a portion of Betty's call on audiotape.

The other flight attendants on the plane relayed information for Betty to report while also trying to keep the passengers safe and as calm as possible during the terrifying flight. Betty Ann Ong and the flight crew of American Airlines Flight 11 were truly professional and heroic for their actions on the plane and in the giving of their lives during the attack on America on Sept.11, 2001.

Courtesy of Rick Ho, *Sing Tao Newspaper*

Zack Zheng is seen briefly in the background of a Fox 5 TV news clip aiding the injured before the Twin Towers collapsed.

Zhe (Zack) Zheng
Heroic Rescuer "So Others May Live"
By Elizabeth R. OuYang

Zhe (Zack) Zheng was only 28 years old. On the morning of September 11, he was working at The Bank of New York near the World Trade Center. After the attack on the Twin Towers, Zack and the rest of his co-workers evacuated their building. However, instead of heading north for safety with the rest of the crowd, Zack headed toward the World Trade Center to volunteer his services as a certified emergency medical technician. He phoned his mother at 9:30 a.m. to inform her that he was fine, but he was going to see if he could help the victims of the attack. He was seen briefly in the background of a Fox 5 TV news clip aiding the injured before the Twin Towers collapsed. That was the last time he was seen or heard from by his family and friends.

Zack emigrated from mainland China to America as a teenager. After graduating from Stuyvesant High School, he received his undergraduate degree and master of business administration from the University of Rochester. While attending the university, he volunteered with the Brighton Volunteer Ambulance from 1995 to 1998. Zack later returned to New York City to help support his mother and brother.

The Brighton Volunteer Ambulance dedicated its new ambulance in memory of Zhe "Zack" Zheng and all the rescuers who died on Sept. 11, 2001, "so others may live."

Zack's grieving mother, Jiaoxian Cen, reflected, "I always taught young people to serve their society and its people. I have lost Zhe, but I am very proud of what he did."

VICTIMS

Many Asian Americans and Pacific Islanders lost their lives in the September 11 attacks. Families of the missing made the transition from mourning their losses to celebrating these lives. They brought together memories and stories as they stood strong for healing and unity.

Courtesy of Madeline Moy

Ted H. Moy was "very patriotic," his wife Madeline says. "He used to buy shirts with flags, flag ties and hats. On Independence Day, he would put on the red, white, and blue."

Teddington Hamm "Ted" Moy
Patriot
By Aryani Ong

On a regularly scheduled workday, Teddington Hamm "Ted" Moy would have been in his office. But Ted, a civilian program manager for information management support at the Pentagon, was being rotated throughout different departments as part of an intensive, one-year training program in the Pentagon's Leadership Development Program. Once completed, he would be eligible to apply for managerial positions within the Pentagon. He was one of only a handful of Pentagon employees who were selected to enter the program. On the morning of September 11, he was two doors down from his office in the Budget and Accounting Department.

Tragically, Ted was one of the 189 people who perished when a hijacked plane crashed into the Pentagon. His co-workers down the hall survived. Ted left behind a wife, daughter Jessica, now 20, and Daniel, 16.

Nearly two years later, Madeline reminisces about the husband whom she met in 1975 at Chien Tan, a culture and language program for overseas Chinese youth in Taiwan. They found they had similar backgrounds. They were born and raised in Chinatowns. He grew up in Washington, D.C.; she hailed from San Francisco. Their families came from the same village in China: Toi Shan in Canton province. They married on a lucky day on the Chinese calendar, July 12, 1980. "He was my life," she said. Throughout their 21 years of marriage, he gave her flowers for all occasions.

"Ted wanted to be what all good Chinese American men want to be: a good son, a good father, a good husband, and a good citizen. He succeeded in all of these things," a family friend, Joseph K. Lee, Jr., wrote to the Moy family after Ted's death. Indeed, Madeline said, her husband "loved God, his family, and America."

"He was a family man," Madeline continued. "He was so supportive of our family. He was protective of us." When Ted

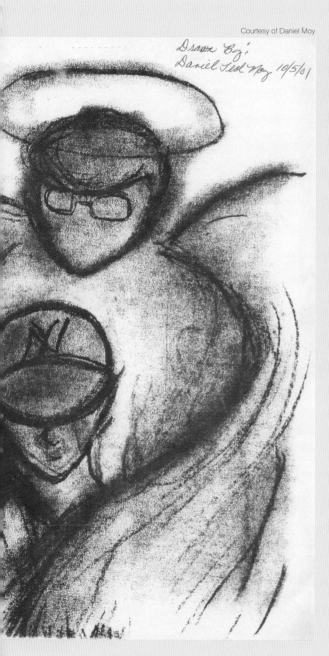

Ted H. Moy's son, Daniel, portrays his father as an angel holding him in an embrace.

died, they lost the "navigator" in the family. Consequently, at times she feels overwhelmed by the daunting task of running the household alone: paying taxes, doing repairs around the house, taking her car to the garage to get fixed. While their daughter Jessica attends college, Madeline is raising their teenage son alone. She wants him to find a college that will cater to his interest in multimedia web programming. But she herself does not know how to research colleges online.

"My son has made the honor roll and made straight As for the last two report cards," she said. "I'm hoping he'll stay motivated to find out which colleges he wants to enter." Ted would have been the one to help his son with college applications.

Madeline finds strength in her husband's devotion to his family. "I feel that I want to do everything the best I can to carry on his name. I am very proud of him and my children," she said. Now, she holds on to the happy memories they had together as a family.

Ted was also involved in his children's activities. "He was very much of a community man," said Madeline. "He helped and volunteered a lot. He was a coordinator of my daughter's string quartet for several years. He always volunteered to help out. When Jessica played her violin with the orchestra, he would feel so enthusiastic and start to dance and bounce and pretend that he was the conductor, conducting the music to that song."

Part of Ted's legacy is the importance he placed on July 4. "He was very patriotic," Madeline said. "He used to buy shirts with flags and flag ties and hats. On Independence Day, he would put on the red, white, and blue." Madeline keeps a photo of him wearing a Dr. Seuss–inspired hat and outfit emblazoned with the flag's stars and stripes. He is pointing his finger as if to say, "I want you to celebrate with me." And his family did.

"He made sure we saw the fireworks because he felt that it was part of celebrating freedom," Madeline said. "He loved the 'Stars and Stripes' song." Ted also told his son that he valued the American eagle because of its symbolism for courage, wisdom, and independence.

"He's like an eagle to me," Ted's wife said.

Michael Kuo(left) poses with his brother Tony(right) and father, Frederick Kuo(center) in 1995. Frederick Kuo, 53, an engineer at Washington Group International, perished in World Trade Tower Two.

Courtesy of Michael Kuo

Frederick Kuo, Jr.
Faithful Church Organizer
By Elizabeth R. OuYang

For more than 20 years, Frederick Kuo, Jr., had worked at an engineering firm in the World Trade Center. At one point, he even successfully fought a job transfer to New Jersey because he loved his view of the harbor and the Statute of Liberty from his Manhattan office on the 91st floor of World Trade Tower Two. He did not survive the September 11 attacks.

After receiving a master's degree in mechanical engineering from Massachuselts Institute of Technology, he and his wife, Dr. Teresita Reyes Kuo, and their four children settled in Great Neck, New York, where Fred was active at the Community Church of Great Neck.

Because of Fred's death, one of his sons, Michael, was unable to focus and almost dropped out of C.U.N.Y. Hunter

College, where he was pursuing a master's degree in urban planning. A teacher encouraged him to apply for a fellowship at the Municipal Art Society (MAS) of New York instead. Michael stayed in school, and now he coordinates a MAS project that helps ordinary people become involved in the planning and memorial process for the World Trade Center site. Organizing more than 200 public workshops in the tri-state region, Michael facilitated the exchange of ideas for the future of the World Trade Center site. Michael fondly remembers his childhood visits to his dad's office and how his father would comment that it was a "marvel of human engineering to build a building that high." By actively participating in the rebuilding process of an area his dad loved, Michael hopes to preserve both his father's spirit and a vision for the future.

56

Courtesy of Nick Ngo

Nancy and Nick pose with their two daughters, Ashley and Lindsay, on vacation. Before Nancy perished in the World Trade Center, their home and two small daughters were the center of their life around which all else revolved.

Nancy Ngo
Family's Cheerleader
By Nick Ngo

The memory of my wife makes me laugh and sometimes makes me cry. I smile and even laugh to myself about precious moments, unforgettable sounds, fun and laughter, craziness that I shared with her. Over the years, Nancy and I have taken many pictures together with our children. In time, I will put all of those pictures into their proper place. This way, our children and I can live in or revisit special places and take time to remember with each other. I can tell stories of their mommy, her life and our lives together. My heart breaks every time I think about our daughters not having Nancy to look up to and grow up with. Nancy had the ability to make them laugh and challenge their physical and intellectual being. She would challenge our older daughter Ashley to bicycling, roller blading, and swimming when Ashley was slightly over four years old. Nancy also had the ability to strongly persuade our daughters that they can accomplish anything if they work hard at it. She would impart values to them that would enable them to be contributors in society when they grow up. Now I would somehow have to instill those attributes that Nancy would be proud of. Nancy had a unique personality and character and was a strong influence in my life. She gave something valuable to me and received from me as well. She came into the world and had an impact, and shall live in my heart and mind forever.

Andrew Jay Hoon Kim
Respected Teacher
By Elizabeth R. OuYang

A Columbia University graduate, Andrew Jay Hoon Kim was most active in teaching youth at the Bethany United Methodist Church in New Jersey and playing guitar and singing at services. He once wrote to the new teachers in charge of the youth, "Please love the kids and be willing to sacrifice anything for them, whether it be your time, your money, or your personal life. Ask how they are doing and get involved with their lives. They say that we can change a life and though some of you don't believe it, it's radically true. I've always considered myself a poor teacher with even poorer relationships with the kids I speak tó but for some, it looks like God has done a miracle with these hands that I've served with. And there is no better feeling."

Andy was 26 years old and working as a certified financial analyst on the 93rd floor of Tower One, World Trade Center, on the day of September 11. While still coping with his personal grief, Andy's father, Paul, within weeks of his son's passing, organized meetings to give emotional and informational support to 18 Korean American families who lost a loved one at the World Trade Center. He also established the Andrew Kim Memorial Foundation, which will give scholarships to high school students Andy mentored at church and to students attending Columbia University.

Paul Kim currently serves as chairman of the Korean Centennial Park Commission, which commemorates 100 years of Korean immigration to the United States. His vision is to erect a memorial for the Korean American victims of the World Trade Center tragedy as part of the park's creation.

© Corky Lee

Paul Kim, in his Laundromat, holds a memorial tribute to his son, Andrew.

Courtesy of Nancy Yamben

Jupiter and Nancy Yamben wear traditional
Indian wedding costumes.

Jupiter Yamben
Proud Immigrant
By Nancy Yamben

Jupiter Yamben's passions included America; his
homeland in Manipur, India; his son Santi; and his wife
Nancy. As the founding member of the North American
Manipur Association in the U.S., Jupiter was very proud
of his culture and wanted to teach Santi all about it. He
worked as a Banquet Manager at Windows on the
World, the famous restaurant on top of the World Trade
Center.

After September 11, Jupiter's family scattered his ashes
at his home on the Hudson River in Beacon, New York;
on Laktok Lake in Manipur; and at his school in the
mountains of Darjeeling, India. To honor Jupiter's
memory, Santi and Nancy participate in all the Meiti
rituals and ceremonies associated with death and
afterlife. In addition, a memorial scholarship is being
established in Jupiter's name at his school in Darjeeling.
Most of all, Santi and Nancy remember "Pa-pa" every
night by blowing him a kiss and saying, "I love you Pa-Pa
and I always will."

Meena Jerath prays in her puja room; a photo of her deceased husband Prem Nath Jerath is in the background.

Prem Nath Jerath
Kind and Thoughtful Man
By Arun Venugopal

Meena Jerath found herself a widow and her son, Neel, without a father on Sept. 11, 2001. The man in their lives, Prem Nath Jerath, was a structural engineer who worked for the Port Authority in the World Trade Center. During the bombing in 1993, Prem had helped a woman walk down 30 flights of stairs.

In the beginning days after Prem's death, said Meena, they had faith in God. She often retreated to the puja room, a converted closet attached to the master bedroom upstairs where she prayed all day. The following summer, she and Neel even went on pilgrimages throughout India, including to Pehowa in Haryana, meant for those whose relatives didn't die a normal death. But it only raised more questions. "You think, 'We did good deeds and we are honest and we'll live a good life,'" she mused. "Why did this happen?"

Courtesy of Seshu Badrinath / Pipal Productions

Amish Sattaluri wishes his deceased mother, Deepika, was here to celebrate his eighth birthday with him.

Deepika Sattaluri
Beloved Mother
By Arun Venugopal

On the wall of the Sattaluri home was a photo of Deepika, smiling as she stood behind her son, Amish, who was sitting in front of his birthday cake. Deepika was a 33-year-old Wipro accountant who worked for Marsh McLennan on the 92nd floor of Tower One. Just two weeks before the attacks on the World Trade Center, Amish's seventh birthday was the family's last occasion together.

The following year, Amish's birthday was a small matter of debate between father and son. Kumar Sattaluri quietly refused Amish's repeated requests for a party. He didn't need to explain why—Amish obviously knew this territory well.

The phone rang, and Amish rushed to pick it up. It was another survivor, a woman who lost her husband. For some, the survivor network has become a surrogate family, often meeting and spending time together. "We don't need to say anything," said Kumar, taking the phone from his son's hands.

Ultimately, Kumar relented to the pressure of other survivors. Amish celebrated his eighth birthday with a party on Aug. 24, 2002.

Swarna Chalasani
Perfect Sari

By Arun Venugopal

Lakshmi Chalasani, sitting in her son's Manhattan apartment, repeatedly returned the conversation to a maroon silk sari when she talked about her late daughter, Swarna. Lakshmi had bought the sari on a trip to Madras, thinking it would be ideal in the event of her daughter meeting a prospective groom. Maroon was her daughter's favorite color. Lakshmi was extremely careful about not buying anything too heavy, knowing full well how her 33-year-old daughter would respond to it.

When Lakshmi returned to New York from Madras, she called up Swarna and described the color, the border, and the design of the sari. "She thought it was much better than those zari saris," said Lakshmi. "She was very good at wearing saris. She carried herself very well, though she didn't have many chances."

One year later, Eva Narula still replays in her mind the commute that her sister, Manika, took to the World Trade Center (WTC). She rationalizes that Manika could not have reached the WTC by the time of the attacks. Here, Narula holds a photo of her deceased younger sister, Manika Narula.

Rao Chalasani posts a flyer of his missing sister, Swarna, on a wall outside of Bellevue Hospital on Sept. 13, 2001. Swarna, a vice president at Fiduciary Trust International, was working on the 94th floor of the World Trade Tower Two on September 11.

Manika Narula
Fondly Remembered Sister
By Arun Venugopal

Eva Narula and her younger sister Manika, or Mona, were like twins, though four years separated them. One year after September 11, Eva still waited for her younger sister to come home any day. After all, she calculated, it was impossible for Mona to have made it to work by 8:48 a.m., when the first World Trade Center tower was hit.

The train pulled into Penn Station at 8:08 a.m., and it took another 20 to 25 minutes to take the subway downtown. On the morning of September 11 though, their train arrived at Penn Station at 8:23 a.m. Eva dashed off without the usual hug. Today, Eva still makes excuses. Mona would have taken her time to make the transfer. And then, once at work, it would have taken her five or ten minutes to fish her ID card out of her handbag. She rationalizes how Mona could have been late to work that day and avoided the tragedy. Of her family's handling of Mona's death, Eva says, "We can't face up to it."

Courtesy of Kenneth and Gloria Chu

Pamela Chu, 31, a vice president at Cantor Fitzgerald, perished in the World Trade Center. Chu was the only Asian trader in her department.

Pamela Chu
Devoted Daughter
By Elizabeth R. OuYang

Pamela Chu was the beloved daughter of Kenneth and Gloria Chu, and a devoted sister to Steven and Miriam Chu. At age two, Pamela came to the United States from Korea. After graduating from college, she went to work for Cantor Fitzgerald. In 10 years, she became Vice President in the Portfolio Trading Group. As on Sept. 11, 2001, she was always punctual for work and was an extremely dedicated employee.

She loved to travel and was an exceptional cook. "Every year for Thanksgiving, Pamela made the turkey and all the trimmings for the entire family. Her aunt and uncle were not particularly fond of turkey, but once they tried Pamela's turkey, their minds changed forever. It will never be the same celebrating the holidays without Pamela," lamented her parents. "She will forever be missed and loved by all of us. Pamela lives in each and every one of our hearts."

Her story has even touched people she never met. Christopher Roche, a soldier in the U.S. Army, read her story in *The New York Times Portrait* and wrote, "I know we will never be able to change what has happened, but please know there are thousands of soldiers like me and marines like my brother, Jon, who are ready, willing and able to risk their lives for Pamela's memory, and it is on our minds daily."

Seong Soon Kang reads his son's favorite passage in the Bible. Seated next to him is Joon Koo's mother, Pil Soon Kang. Standing are two of Joon Koo's sisters, Rebecca Hoang and Jamie Kang.

Joon Koo Kang
Pillar of the Family
By Elizabeth R. OuYang

Saying good-bye to his wife and two young daughters, Joon Koo Kang left his home in New Jersey at 5:50 a.m. on Sept. 11, 2001. His destination was the 104th floor of Tower One, where he worked as a systems analyst for Cantor Fitzgerald. He made it to work as usual, but has never made it back home again.

Born in South Korea, Joon Koo immigrated to the United States with his parents and three younger sisters. As the oldest child and only son of Mr. and Mrs. Seong Soon Kang, he was the pillar of the family. With traditional working-class parents reaching retirement, Joon Koo helped to support them. He was active in his church, often traveling on missionary trips. Every night, he faithfully read the Bible to his children. Despite his many responsibilities, Joon Koo still found time to play his saxophone. At age 34, Joon Koo died, a devoted son, husband, and father.

$\mathcal{V}$ICTIMS

Courtesy of Rui Zheng

Yuguang Zheng, a retired chemist, and Shuyin Yang, a retired pediatrician, were aboard American Airlines Flight 77 when it was hijacked and flown into the Pentagon. They were returning to China after visiting their daughter in Maryland. The photo shows the couple visiting the Liberty Bell in Philadelphia.

Shuyin Yang and Yuguang Zheng
Loving Parents
By Rui Zheng

I had an extremely close relationship with my parents. They always made time and did their best for my brother and me. My mother would stop whatever she was doing and give us her undivided attention when we needed assistance or advice. My father encouraged us and challenged us to succeed, and disciplined us fairly. He was kind, compassionate, and the most positive person that I have ever known in my life. He was my anchor. Mom not only gave life to me, but also was my close friend. There was absolutely nothing that I could not share with her. I have indeed been blessed with some of the most wonderful parents in the world.

Since their tragic deaths, my world has been so empty without them. I miss them more than mere words can ever convey. Sometimes just looking at their pictures brings back a flood of memories and the teardrops start. I miss their smiles, their laughter, their love, their hugs, their strength, their support, and their advice when things were difficult for me. One of my most cherished memories of them is seeing them waiting for me in front of my apartment building every evening when they lived with me in the last year of their lives. Even now, sometimes when I approach my apartment, I still have a feeling that they are standing there waiting for me, like the old days. Death can end our physical connections, but the bonds are still there.

The...enormous impact on the lives of people....

CHAPTER 5

HOMELAND SECURITY

Former NYPD Deputy Chief Dewey Fong (second left) joins other rescuers at the Opening Bell of the New York Stock Exchange on Sept. 19, 2001.

Courtesy of New York Stock Exchange

"The...enormous impact on the lives of people will forever be carried in the hearts of all."

Dewey Fong
Former Deputy Chief, New York Police Department
By Dewey Fong

In the face of an unprecedented crisis, former Deputy Chief Dewey Fong quickly acted to mobilize police resources under his command at the New York Police Department Patrol Borough Queens South to ensure public safety at the World Trade Center. He coordinated the closing of all highways in Queens County to facilitate emergency responses and managed an emergency plan to control access to and from John F. Kennedy International Airport. He deployed police officers to security checkpoints at

Queens-Manhattan tunnels and bridges for emergency vehicle access to aid in rescue operations. Adjacent to the disaster area in the lower tip of Manhattan, Fong also established an on-scene command post to coordinate rescue and security operations as well as logistical support. For a protracted period during the operations, he led by example and concerned himself with the safety and well being of all emergency personnel who were surrounded by unstable buildings, underground fires, contaminated air, and other dangerous hazards.

"The savage effects of this terrorist act against the people of the United States and its enormous impact on the lives of people touched by its destructive intent will forever be carried in the hearts of all who witnessed the suffering during the rescue and recovery efforts," Fong said.

"Come to the White House immediately."

Norman Mineta
Secretary, U.S. Department of Transportation
By David Louie

I was in Nashville on the morning of September 11, attending a board meeting of the Radio Television News Directors Association. That afternoon, I was on the road to Washington to cover the attack on the Pentagon. I spent the next two weeks doing live reports to San Francisco with the crash site behind me. The scene was ghastly. It was also surreal, especially at night as recovery teams searched the rubble around the clock, first for survivors, then for the dead, in the glare of floodlights. TV crews and satellite trucks from every network and from dozens of stations across the country set up camp on a knoll behind a gas station.

It hit me—and my news director 3,000 miles away—that we were missing a historic element of this tragic event. There was a Cabinet member with Bay Area roots just across the Potomac who was facing awesome decisions, a man with extraordinary experience, insight, and perspective.

I had Norman Mineta's home telephone number in my pocket organizer. I placed a call, hoping to reach Mineta over the weekend when the maelstrom of events might slow down. I left a message on his answering machine.

That evening, while my photographer and I were grabbing a fast-food dinner

Courtesy of David Louie and KGO-TV

KGO-TV reporter David Louie reports live from the Pentagon after it was hit by a terrorist attack.

in between live reports to the West Coast, my cell phone rang. It was Mineta's press secretary, Chet Lunner. Arrangements were made to carve out 10 minutes for an exclusive, one-on-one interview with the Secretary the next day, a Sunday, following a not-yet-announced press conference. The federal government was operating in overdrive, working nonstop to secure the nation's transportation network from additional attacks. It was an opportunity to talk with Mineta as he was facing the greatest challenges of his career. He was responsible for commercial aviation, highways and roads, rail networks, public transit, pipelines, seaports, and domestic waterways—all suddenly vulnerable.

It would be easy to ask Mineta the nuts-and-bolts questions, but what I really wanted was to capture and share his feelings, reactions, and response to the horrific events of September 11.

I covered Mineta's press conference, where he announced the creation of two advisory task forces. I had to watch for a signal from an aide to break from the throng of reporters. Photographer Guy Hall and I were to rendezvous with Mineta in a back hallway, then take a private elevator with him to his office.

In Mineta's private office, we discussed critical issues he had to address: how to reinforce cockpit doors, whether the government should take over airport security screening from the airlines, how to restore public confidence in flying, and the financial impact of shutting

Secretary of Transportation Norman Mineta took less than three hours to ground 5,000 aircraft on September 11.

Courtesy of David Louie and KGO-TV

"The...enormous impact on the lives of people will forever be carried in the hearts of all."

"Come to the White House immediately."

"My hope is that September 11 restored a sense of a larger purpose in life and perhaps even inspired patriotism in some."

" You can fly the airplane...without being a citizen. But you can't check the bags of the passengers."

down the nation's airspace. I brought up the personal stake he had in airline safety. His wife, Deni, is a retired United Airlines flight attendant. A son and stepson are commercial airline pilots.

We moved to his office, where a flat-panel monitor sat on the credenza behind his desk. It displayed dots for every aircraft in U.S. airspace. About 5,000 aircraft were in the skies on the day of September 11. It took less than three hours to ground them.

Mineta recalled how the government's rapid response began with a chilling phone call from the Vice President's office: "Come to the White House immediately." Response to acts of terrorism required swift, decisive action. However, the implications were not lost on the President and his Cabinet with Mineta seated at the table. Mineta said the President was very sensitive about the potential for backlash aimed at citizens of Middle Eastern ancestry.

"We don't want that to happen because we don't want what happened to Norm Mineta to happen again," President Bush said. Mineta experienced the sting of injustice and discrimination early in life. When he was 10 years old, Mineta was one of 120,000 Japanese Americans sent to camps because of Executive Order 9066, a product of wartime hysteria.

History had not been forgotten, thanks to the experience of Mineta from San Jose who grew up to be a highly visible and respected member of the President's inner circle.

"My hope is that September 11 restored a sense of a larger purpose in life and perhaps even inspired patriotism in some."

H.K. Park
Former Deputy Assistant,
Secretary of Defense for Civil Support
By Aryani Ong

Even before Sept. 11, 2001, H.K. Park, 32, was no stranger to the idea of terrorist attacks on U.S. soil. Having worked at the Pentagon until January 2001 as Deputy Assistant to the Secretary of Defense for Civil Support, he had planned for scenarios where the U.S. military would assist state and city governments respond to chemical, biological, and nuclear attacks. He knew the challenges involved: Quarantine a city. Decontaminate a stadium. Set up military field hospitals in city parks. Fortunately, no chemical, biological, or nuclear weapons were used during that day's attacks.

On the morning of September 11, he learned the news from a receptionist who interrupted his conference call about a trip to the Middle East he was planning with his boss the following week. Park's boss: former Secretary of Defense William Cohen, who served under President Clinton. After the Bush administration entered office, Park followed Cohen to form his new political risk consulting group.

"I was very surprised," Park said, about his own reaction to the attacks. "However, I knew how the federal government would continue operating. Key people would be moved to secure locations and other plans would be set in motion. It gave me a peace of mind."

He checked on his former colleagues at the Pentagon. Even after the plane had crashed into one side of the Pentagon, some employees were unaware of the attack. The sprawling building had insulated the noise from certain sectors where 23,000 employees worked.

After the call, Park then made his own preparations. "We went out and bought a lot of sandwiches," Park said. "We knew people would panic. I knew it would be a long day of traffic, and that it would be safer to stay in the office than to go home."

For the American public, September 11 was a wake-up call. But for Park, the government has been taking homeland security issues seriously for years.

"There has been real effort and money invested by the Department of Defense and other federal agencies to prepare for terrorist attacks," Park said. "But prior to September 11, it was difficult to convince Congress, the media, and the public that the effort was worthwhile. We were often accused of being Chicken Little."

Since that day, Park has been lecturing to student groups and professional organizations on the range of terrorist threats that we face and how the government is preparing. His firm, The Cohen Group, has also been advising companies on which technologies can best support Homeland Security. Besides public support for budgetary increases for homeland security, Park hopes that the tragedy will bring about another change.

Courtesy of H.K. Park

Former Deputy Assistant to the Secretary of Defense for Civil Support, H.K. Park used to plan responses for terrorist attack scenarios at the Pentagon. Now, he provides political risk advice to companies operating internationally.

"For many of us, our parents migrated to this country. Our generation has thrived in the U.S., but few have had a chance to give back to this country," Park said. "My hope is that September 11 restored a sense of a larger purpose in life and perhaps even inspired patriotism in some. Although we represent just four percent of the population, we have so much more to offer this nation."

$\mathcal{H}$OMELAND SECURITY

Courtesy of David Bacon

Airport screeners attend a rally against anti-immigrant legislation in front of the Federal Building in San Francisco on Feb. 26, 2003.

"You can fly the airplane...without being a citizen. But you can't check the bags of the passengers."

Erlinda Valencia
Airport Baggage Screener
By David Bacon and Lillian Galedo

Erlinda Valencia came from the Philippines almost two decades ago. Like many Filipino immigrants living in the San Francisco Bay Area, she found a job at the airport, screening passengers' baggage. For most of the 14 years Valencia was there, she held a minimum-wage job; she could barely support her family working 40 hours a week. Then, two years ago, organizers from the Service Employees International Union (SEIU) began talking to the screeners. Valencia decided to get involved, and eventually became a leader in the campaign that brought in the union. "We were very happy," she remembered. "It seemed to us all

that for the first time, we had a real future."

Then September 11 happened. In the name of national security and anti-terrorism, the rights and livelihoods of airport screeners were taken away immediately following the tragic terrorist attacks. The passage of the Aviation and Transportation Security Act (ATSA) on Nov. 19, 2001, required the federalization of airport screeners. It also mandated that the screeners be U.S. citizens. As a result, approximately 30,000 screeners, working in every major metropolitan area, were fired in

70

one of the single-largest mass terminations ever. Those who lost their jobs were mostly immigrants and minorities.

Along with screeners nationwide, Valencia was caught up in a wave of anti-immigrant legislation and repression that profoundly affected immigrants and workers across the country in the wake of September 11. Non-citizens were instantly ineligible to occupy these positions and incumbent screeners who were citizens were required to re-apply for their positions. When the government unfolded their transition plan in the summer of 2002, the centerpiece of the re-application process was an eight-hour assessment that was heavily reliant on passing a computerized examination that was one-third English language competency and two-thirds "psychological fitness/aptitude." The failure rate among incumbent screeners was 80 to 85 percent. This resulted in the massive lay-off of thousands of workers nationally, including approximately 1,200 in the San Francisco Bay Area.

Immigrants and workers of color were systematically excluded from jobs that, prior to September 11, had been held by a predominantly minority workforce at the top 100 airports where 80 percent of the screeners were employed. After passing ATSA, the Transportation Security Administration (TSA) reported that the workforce was 61 percent white. Of the original 30,000 screeners, only around 4,500 were rehired.

In the San Francisco Bay Area, Filipino workers (who made up approximately 70 percent of the screener workforce) were hit particularly hard by the passage of ATSA. Many of the screeners—citizens and non-citizens alike—had served in these jobs for many years, some for more than 10 years. "It's so unfair," Valencia said. "I've done this job for 14 years, and we're all really good at it. Instead of wanting us to continue, they hired people with no experience at all, and we had to train them, too. You can fly the airplane, even if you're not a citizen, and you can carry a rifle in the airport as a member of the National Guard doing security without being a citizen, either. But you can't check the bags of the passengers."

Today, airport screeners and their families are living on the threshold of poverty. Some of the screeners have multiple family members who lost their jobs. Many screeners over the age of 60 (some in their 70s) will have an extremely difficult time finding employment. The majority is on unemployment, averaging $1,200 each month ($14,400 annual income). For many, their benefits will run out in the next few months, if they haven't already.

Screeners and their allies in the San Francisco Bay Area continue to fight for the reinstatement of the unemployed screeners. Screeners have organized their own worker organization, dubbed People's Association of Workers and Immigrant Screeners, to advocate for the return of their jobs. Ironically, the government is accepting applications for part-time screener positions, requiring a minimum of one year of screener experience to apply. Grudgingly, some of the out-of-work screeners are applying; many others are cautiously waiting to see what happens.

CHAPTER 6

TRIBUTE AND REMEMBRANCE

A symbolic candlelight vigil is held under the Kim Lao Memorial Arch in Chatham Square, Chinatown. The memorial was dedicated to a Chinese American aviator who lost his life fighting during World War II.

>

© Corky Lee

© Corky Lee

In Flushing, Queens, where a large concentration of Chinese Americans, Korean Americans, and South Asian Americans reside, onlookers observe a candlelight vigil outside Flushing Queens Library.

^

© Corky Lee

their loved ones.

The Tibetan people have strong commitment to the principles of non-violence.

We pray especially that New Yorkers will find the strength in their hearts to come through this difficult time with a deep spirit of compassion, tolerance, love and patience.

In Union Square Park in Manhattan, less than three miles from the site of the World Trade Center, a Buddhist prayer vigil and candlelight ceremony takes place. Organized by the New York-New Jersey Tibetan Buddhist community, the vigil is open to the public to chant for peace and the souls of people killed by the September 11 attacks.

^

*T*RIBUTE & REMEMBRANCE

People across the nation held candlelight vigils, built memorials and sent letters to firehouses conveying love and respect for days following the World Trade Center attacks. The outpouring of support and caring were expressed through the flowers, teddy bears, candles, photos, and notes placed at makeshift shrines.

© Corky Lee

On Sept. 15, 2001, the tri-state Sikh community holds a candlelight vigil in Central Park, drawing 2,500 people. By praying openly for the victims, it sends an important message to the public that the Sikh community condemns terrorism. Among the concerned that attend is a young Sikh girl from Queens. Undergoing radiation for leukemia, she has no hair and is in a wheelchair. Wanting to show her support for her community, she pleaded with her father to let her be there.

A makeshift memorial is erected at Chatham Square in Chinatown.

Courtesy of Jami Gong

74

People mourn and gather for vigils in Union Square after the attack on the World Trade Center. A man writes in Chinese "World Peace" on the pavement.

TRIBUTE & REMEMBRANCE

Jinnie Yun, a student at New York
University, lights a candle at a service
held in New York's Washington Square
Park on Sept. 12, 2001.

^

>

Northwest Airlines flight crewmember Nick Sengchanh
bows his head in prayer while waiting for a flight to
Detroit as airport personnel and passengers hold hands
in the atrium at Hartsfield International Airport in Atlanta,
Georgia, on Sept. 14, 2001. The day has been declared
a "National Day of Prayer and Remembrance" following
the September 11 terrorist attacks.

76

Young people gather in New York's Times Square for a candlelight vigil on Sept. 14, 2001.

TRIBUTE & REMEMBRANCE

Local Chinese American residents gather for a candlelight vigil on Oct. 5, 2001.

^

TRIBUTE & REMEMBRANCE

In Union Square, a woman looks at photos of the missing on Sept. 17, 2001. A banner with Chinese and English messages calls for "World Peace."

<

A makeshift memorial in Union Square is illuminated by hundreds of candles and notes.

An inter-faith memorial service is held to honor the victims of the September 11 attacks.

Buddhists chant for peace at a memorial service on 14th Street in New York City on Sept. 21, 2001.

President George W. Bush (second from right), New York Mayor Rudolph W. Guiliani (first from left), and Governor George Pataki (second from left) join the first grade class of teacher Debra Nelson (center) in a recitation of the Pledge of Allegiance on Oct. 3, 2001, at DeSoto Public School in New York's Chinatown, near the site of the World Trade Center destruction.

TRIBUTE & REMEMBRANCE

TRIBUTE & REMEMBRANCE

An observance is held at Ground Zero to mark the first anniversary of the terrorist attacks and to honor those who died at the World Trade Center. Hundreds of Asian Americans and Pacific Islanders lost their lives during the attacks on the World Trade Center.

Family members and others gather at Ground Zero where the Twin Towers of the World Trade Center once stood. They come to lay flowers to honor the memory of the victims on Sept. 11, 2002.

Despite facing the challenge of rebuilding....

The collapse of the World Trade Center and its aftermath had an enormous impact on the Asian American and Pacific Islander community. Over 100 people of Asian descent lost their lives in the World Trade Center. Due to its proximity to Ground Zero, Chinatown was caught in the declared "frozen zone," barricaded from the public for days while the rescue effort was ongoing. Asian Americans and Pacific Islanders living in the five boroughs of New York or commuting from New Jersey and working in Manhattan were faced with the sudden loss of jobs and markedly decreased earnings. Restaurant, garment, hotel, and construction workers, service personnel, and taxi drivers were all affected by the decrease in business and tourism activity. Public transportation, street cleaning, and phone service were shut down for days and even months in parts of Chinatown.

In addition to the acute financial losses, the emotional impact took a significant toll on the community. Family members, survivors, and co-workers were all directly impacted by the tragedy and in need of crisis counseling. From a mere10 blocks away, thousands of Chinatown residents witnessed the Twin Towers burning and collapsing. Adding to the high level of stress were the dangers from falling debris and from the variety of toxins, smoke, and dust residents were exposed to. The billowing smoke and hazardous fumes blew across the river to Brooklyn and Queens, uptown throughout Manhattan, and lingered in the air for months.

There was an urgent need to address these issues before federal relief agencies could respond. The problems were further compounded by federal and charity relief agencies' guidelines for providing assistance. Nearly 45 percent of Chinatown residents live north of Canal Street, a major thoroughfare, yet relief efforts were being restricted to those living south of Canal Street. Moreover, many of those who did live south of Canal Street were also disqualified. Because Chinatown and other immigrant groups rely on a cash economy, which does not translate into formal receipts and documented evidence, many affected by the World Trade Center disaster were denied relief. In addition, certain occupations were listed as qualifying for relief and others were not. The taxi industry, largely composed of South Asian American drivers, was initially denied economic relief even though its livelihood is heavily dependent on Wall Street, World Trade Center, and airport activity.

The location of relief centers outside the community and the lack of culturally sensitive services, including a shortage of translators and bilingual outreach materials on eligibility requirements and types of relief, greatly limited community access to these services. Other mounting issues included lack of access to health and legal services to help those affected maneuver within bureaucracies.

Faced with these formidable obstacles, community groups united to respond.

Courtesy of Chenghui Hsu, *World Journal*

Chinatown After September 11:
An Economic Impact Study

Below are some of the key findings of a study entitled "Chinatown After September 11," released on April 4, 2002, by the Asian American Federation of New York (AAFNY):

1. Thousands of workers lost their jobs or suffered severely reduced hours.
2. In the first two weeks after September 11, nearly three out of every four Chinatown workers were temporarily dislocated. Businesses in the garment, restaurant, retail, and tourism industries suffered revenue declines ranging from 60 percent to 100 percent.
3. Three months after September 11, nearly 25 percent of the workforce–some 7,700 workers–was still unemployed. Many of these workers were in the garment and restaurant industries.

In the wake of the September 11 attacks, AAFNY established the World Trade Center Fund, collecting $420,000 to assist families of direct victims and affected workers. It also procured financial support of more than $3.8 million for a number of Asian American and Pacific Islander community agencies and its own relief activities. With this money, AAFNY established relief service projects with partner agencies to serve different Asian American and Pacific Islander communities in Manhattan and Queens, including a relief and recovery site in Queens to meet the ongoing September 11–related needs in South Asian American, Korean American, and other communities. The six partner agencies include Asian American Federation of New York-Queens Office, Chinatown YMCA, Chinese-American Planning Council, Filipino American Human Services, Japanese American Social Services, Inc. and New York Asian Women's Center.

Over 5,000 affected residents in New York's Chinatown wait for relief assistance on a rainy day in Columbus Park, December 2001.

HARDSHIP & SOLIDARITY

Despite facing the challenge of rebuilding New York's Chinatown, communities found strength and came together in times of crisis.

© Corky Lee

Tony Wong, shown here, is the General Manager of AM 1480. In the background is a framed Chinese American newspaper article of Tony Wong presenting Mayor Giuliani a check for $1,094,292.97, along with a list of all the people who contributed and the amounts of their donations.

HARDSHIP & SOLIDARITY

The Power of Chinese American Solidarity

By Elizabeth R. Ou Yan g

AM 1480 is one of more than 30 community-based radio stations across the country owned by Yvonne Liu and her husband Arthur, founders of Sinocast and Sino Television, successful Chinese American radio and television services. As the only Chinese-Cantonese AM station in New York City, non-English-speaking Chinese New Yorkers relied on AM 1480 as a critical source of news and updates on the World Trade Center disaster. During the horrific attacks, AM 1480 remained on the air, providing nonstop coverage from less than one mile away from Ground Zero. With 80 percent of the programming involving live listener call-ins, AM 1480 provided a needed outlet for Chinese-speaking Americans who wanted to express their sorrow, outrage, and sympathy. Within two days of the attack, AM 1480, Sinocast, and Sino Television launched a fundraising campaign to assist the city's relief efforts. Over 60,000 listeners made donations and more than 8,000 letters flooded the station. People lined the streets outside AM 1480, including one 86-year-old Chinese American man who walked 45 minutes to the station to hand deliver a $1 donation to Liu. This successful two-week campaign raised over $1.45 million, of which $375,000 was donated to the Red Cross and more than $1 million went to the Twin Towers Fund, a fund established by former New York Mayor Rudy Giuliani to aid the families of victims. "It was a very gratifying feeling to see so many Chinese Americans showing their compassion for fellow New Yorkers and pride in America through their donations," said Liu.

87

ENGLISH TRANSLATION OF LETTER SINOCAST RECEIVED

"Thank you very much for AM 1480, DJ and all your workers. Originally, we could send money to different organizations, but we wanted the rest of America to know that the Chinese in America make contributions just like the other racial groups. We love America just like everyone else. We are not outsiders. We collect all the contributions so we can show the power of Chinese solidarity and our determination to live and die for this country because we feel if we do that, we can have a lasting impact. This is why we are giving the donation to you. Please accept it. We are donating money, but please do not announce our name on the radio. We do not want to make a name for ourselves because of this disaster."

ENGLISH TRANSLATION OF LETTER SINOCAST RECEIVED

"I'm helping an 83-year-old lady who sends a greeting to you. This elderly lady says that ever since the World Trade Center disaster, she felt very sad. She feels very sorry she cannot help out more because she is too old. She asks me to send you a $50 donation to your radio station. Please accept it on her behalf. . . ."

88

ENGLISH TRANSLATION OF LETTER SINOCAST RECEIVED

"First, I would like to congratulate you. I hope all is well. Every day I listen to your radio station and feel great comfort in listening to your station. I especially appreciate all your help in fundraising for the 9/11 tragedy. When 9/11 happened, I was so frightened. I was crying because my daughter was in the World Trade Center, but luckily she escaped the disaster and came home safely. I'm so grateful, but I'm so saddened and angry by all the policemen and firemen who died. That's why my husband and I are giving this $100 donation. It is so little, but we wanted to show our condolences. We are both over 70, retired and dependent on social security. I hope the masses of Chinese Americans will please give so that relatives of people who sacrificed their lives will feel supported. I don't write well, please forgive me."

Workers attend a rally led by the Chinese Staff and Workers' Association in Foley Square, New York City.

Workers Cry for Unmet Needs

By Elizabeth R. OuYang

In the three months following September 11, more than 3,000 workers, largely limousine drivers, restaurant employees, and garment workers who worked in Chinatown north of Canal Street, flooded the Chinese Staff and Workers' Association (CSWA) for help. Teaming with other worker advocacy groups, CSWA led a grassroots campaign to overturn the stringent standards of eligibility set by federal relief agencies. Through community surveys, town hall meetings, and multiple rallies in New York City and Washington, D.C., Federal Emergency Management Agency (FEMA), state

agencies, and other charity groups responded by extending relief to geographical locations north of Canal Street and beyond. These changed guidelines led to an additional $3.8 million in relief funds to aid impacted workers in the area. Under new standards of eligibility, more displaced workers qualified for state health plans. Eligibility for FEMA air purifiers and vacuum cleaners was extended to affected residents living in the five boroughs of New York City.

A Major Victory for South Asian
American Taxi Drivers
By Elizabeth R. OuYang

With a work force of predominantly South Asian American and other Third World immigrants, the taxi industry received a double blow. In the months following the September 11 attacks, the "frozen zone" imposed in Lower Manhattan and the closing of La Guardia and John F. Kennedy airports and bridges sharply reduced tourism to Manhattan. For weeks, taxi drivers lost substantial income, given that 70 percent of their fares are from Manhattan near the World Trade Center.

To add to their sudden misfortune, the Federal Emergency Management Agency (FEMA) was only giving monetary assistance to qualifying individuals and businesses located south of Canal Street. Undeterred, the drivers appeared before a diverse panel of representatives from federal and government agencies, charities, and community-based groups, testifying to the impact of September 11 on the taxi industry at a public hearing organized by New York Taxi Workers Alliance (NYTWA). With unrelenting drive to keep their plight in the public eye, NYTWA convinced FEMA to change its guidelines. Yellow Cab drivers are now eligible for mortgage and rental assistance if they experienced a minimum 25 percent loss of income since September 11 and had rent arrears or feared eviction. This was a major victory for the drivers.

Courtesy of New York Taxi Workers Alliance

A public hearing on the impact of September 11 on the taxi industry is organized by New York Taxi Workers Alliance.

Courtesy of Yujian Liu, *Coastide Magazine*

The collapse of the World Trade Center Towers sent a variety of toxins into the air, including asbestos. Here, a concerned resident covered with a mask catches up on news about the rescue mission at Ground Zero.

Asthma Toll in Chinatown
Continues To Rise
By Elizabeth R. OuYang

Air quality has become a growing health concern among Chinatown residents. The collapse of the Twin Towers sent a variety of toxins into the air, including asbestos. Dust from the falling debris and strong smells of burning rubber lingered in the air as the World Trade Center continued to burn for days. This further exacerbated the poor air quality problem in Chinatown, which has one of the highest levels of diesel pollution in New York City caused by heavy traffic, ongoing road and bridge work, and outdoor construction.

Since poor air quality contributes to asthma, Chinatown Progressive Association (CPA) conducted a survey to determine the magnitude of the asthma problem in the spring 2002. The survey included 580 households in Chinatown, representing 2,040 individuals. The results revealed that one in five households have an asthma problem. School age children comprised 51 percent of the people with asthma. Half of these cases were diagnosed after the World Trade Center collapse.

A Chinese newspaper article in *World Journal* chronicles the impact of emotional distress on New York's Chinatown communities. Four months after September 11, a survey conducted by the Charles B. Wang Community Health Center reveals 48 percent of Chinatown residents show major symptoms of emotional distress.

The Hamilton Madison House conducted educational outreach programs on post-traumatic stress disorder at garment factories, union meetings, family associations, schools, and street fairs. Here, New York's Chinatown residents are reading in-language educational materials on how to cope with stress and trauma.

Emotional Distress Also a Concern

By Elizabeth R. OuYang and Icy Smith

The Charles B. Wang Community Health Center (CWCHC) and the Hamilton Madison House (HMH) took on new challenges following the aftermath of September 11 in meeting the mental health needs of its residents. To identify the extent of people with post-traumatic stress disorder, the CWCHC conducted 500 bilingual surveys throughout the community. During the first few weeks after September 11, the results showed 69 percent of Chinatown residents with major symptoms of emotional distress. The HMH recruited in-language counselors to conduct educational outreach on post-traumatic stress disorder. Since December 2001, 35,000 people have been helped at HMH. Seventy percent of the patients were from the Chinese American community. The problems included nightmares, hyper vigilance and hypersensitivity, anger, and depression. People feared relocating back to Chinatown and felt the need to talk to others. Victims' families also felt emotional trauma.

To respond to the crisis, the CWCHC has provided low-cost health care to people who lost their health benefits as a result of losing their jobs or businesses from the impact of September 11. Since the program started in August 2002, more than 1,000 people have enrolled in their health care program.

93

Elaine Chao (center), U.S. Secretary of Labor, visits New York's Chinatown. On Dec. 1, 2001, Chao announces a million-dollar emergency grant to aid Chinatown workers left jobless after the September 11 terrorist acts. "The attacks of September 11 have battered Chinatown's usually thriving economy," Chao said.

© Corky Lee

Jack Chung (center) assists the owners of Win Hop Restaurant.

Win Hop Restaurant Faces Possibility of Closing

A recent City University of New York (CUNY) law school graduate, and a business advisor for the Small Business Development Center at LaGuardia Community College/CUNY, Jack Chung helped save Win Hop Restaurant, located in the heart of Chinatown, from closing after the devastating impact of September 11. Moved by an article in the *Sing Tao Newspaper* about how Tim Ho, one of the restaurant's owners, made multiple attempts to apply for a Small Business Administration (SBA) loan and was denied on minor technical grounds, Chung reached out to help the restaurant owners. Guiding them through the bureaucratic hurdles, he was successful in helping them secure a $70,500 loan from SBA. As a result, the restaurant was able to pay its employees and stay in business.

© Corky Lee

94

Courtesy of Yujian Liu, Coastside Magazine

Most businesses on Canal Street, one of the
thriving business districts in Chinatown, are closed.
The local Chinatown economy has been hit hard.
Three months after September 11, 7,700 workers
are still out of work.

A Dedicated and Tireless Translator

By Elizabeth R. OuYang

Veronica Jung was all set to start as a first-year associate with a law firm in Washington, D.C. However, the terrorist
attack on the World Trade Center made a smooth transition from New York to Washington, D.C. impossible.
Responding to an emergency call by the Red Cross for Korean translators, Jung headed for the Family Assistance
Center at Pier 94. She was assigned to help Korean-speaking parents of victims killed in the Twin Towers collapse.
Unaware of the magnitude of the volunteer role she had undertaken, Jung assumed the place of the lost child, who in
normal circumstances would have served as the person helping these elderly, monolingual parents. Instinctively, Jung
began escorting them to Ground Zero for private viewings, helping them file for death certificates, interpreting for
them at family grief-counseling sessions, translating government documents, and filling out emergency aid
applications. After she moved to Washington, D.C., Jung continued to return to New York City on the weekends to
help these families. Eventually, Jung moved back to New York City.

Veronica Jung translates
English to Korean for Mr.
and Mrs. Seong Soon
Kang, parents of Joon
Koo Kang, who was killed
in the World Trade Center
collapse.

© Corky Lee

Signs of "Welcome to Chinatown" are seen along streets in New York's Chinatown. Chinese Consolidated Benevolent Association plays an important role in promoting "Welcome Back to Chinatown, We're Open for Business" campaign.

Welcome Back to Chinatown, We're Open for Business
By Elizabeth R. OuYang and Icy Smith

Chinatown residents were directly affected in the first six months following September 11, but few were going to the Federal Emergency Management Assistance (FEMA) Relief Center for help. Community groups such as the Chinese-American Planning Council (CPC) and the Chinese Consolidated Benevolent Association (CCBA) organized hundreds of bilingual translators and volunteers to provide assistance to more than 4,000 Chinatown and Lower Manhattan residents whose needs had fallen through the cracks.

The wide array of services provided included immediate counseling, visiting homebound seniors who were isolated from disconnected phones and television services, and helping small community businesses and individuals overcome cultural and language barriers in applying for FEMA and other federal relief assistance.

CCBA helped restore businesses in Chinatown by launching advertising campaigns with the theme of "Welcome Back to Chinatown, We're Open for Business." Since sanitation services had been severely reduced in the weeks following September 11, street cleaning was one of their rebuilding efforts.

To identify the current needs in Chinatown, Asian Americans For Equality (AAFE) took a leadership role in the Rebuild Chinatown Initiative. After surveying nearly 2,000 Chinatown residents, workers, and community leaders and holding community meetings, at the top of their list of concerns were employment and income generation, affordable housing, senior housing, and sanitation. With support from the U.S. Department of Labor and other local agencies, CPC has expanded its job training and ESL classes to displaced workers, primarily in the garment industry, to obtain clerical, apparel design, and hotel jobs.

HARDSHIP & SOLIDARITY

Asian Americans for Equality (AAFE) has taken a leadership role in the Rebuild Chinatown Initiative (RCI) to cope with the crisis. Photo from left to right: Andy Liu, VP of Asian American Business Network Corp.; Christopher Kui, Executive Director, AAFE; Congresswoman Nydia Velazquez and Jim Park, Vice President of Industry Relations and Housing Outreach, Freddie Mac, address the community needs in the RCI Conference on July 8, 2002.

Courtesy of Asian Americans for Equality

Courtesy of Chinese-American Planning Council

A garment worker attends an apparel training program run by the Chinese-American Planning Council in hopes of getting a better paying job with a fashion house in New York City. An official from the September 11 Fund reported that 8,000 garment workers lost their jobs and 146 garment factories closed during the 16 months following the September 11 attacks.

An Unrelenting Rescue from Chinese-American Planning Council

A young Chinese immigrant, a student in a job training class in Chinatown, was injured during the crowded frenzy to flee the area once news of the World Trade Center collapse spread. The young woman was thrown to the pavement during the ensuing panic, falling on her face. Seconds later, two others fell on top of her. She sustained facial lacerations, injuries to her neck, and significant damage to her jaws and teeth. None of the mainstream relief agencies would help defray her medical expenses because she was in the emergency room for only 12 hours, half of the 24 hours required to qualify for aid. She was also found ineligible for other relief funds because she neither lived nor worked below Canal Street, but simply studied there. It was Chinese-American Planning Council 9/11 Relief Services, funded through the Federation of Protestant Welfare Agencies and by The New York Times Neediest Fund, that came to her rescue and paid her medical bills.

© Corky Lee

Potri Manis returns to duty at Cabrini Medical Hospital on the morning of September 11 after hearing the shocking news of the World Trade Center attack. Manis treats injured policemen and pours saline in people's eyes at Ground Zero. Days later, Manis performed with Kinding Sindaw, a Filipino American dance group, at interfaith peace rallies in New York City.

<

Courtesy of Yujian Liu, *Coastide Magazine*

>

Four Chinese American garment workers in Chinatown display American flags along Canal Street. Thousands of garment workers were left jobless in the months following September 11.

Businesses on the south end of Canal Street are paralyzed. Chinatown's small businesses were devastated after September 11 because of street closures and loss of tourism. Police are blocking traffic in and out of Centre and Canal Streets.

<

$\mathcal{H}$ARDSHIP & SOLIDARITY

>

Residents of Battery Park City in Lower Manhattan leave their homes with a small selection of their belongings after being allowed to return briefly to retrieve their possessions on Sept. 15, 2001.

Board members and supporters of the San Diego Chapter of the Organization of Chinese Americans(OCA) sing "God Bless America" at a disaster-relief fundraiser titled "Love Our America" on Oct. 11, 2001.

Photos of the Twin Towers are sold for 50 cents each on Walker Street. Funds are used to assist the victims' families.

© Corky Lee

The neighborhood memorial wall murals constructed by Chinese American residents are prominently displayed at Madison Street and James Street in Lower Manhattan. The mural is an innovative project of the Lower Manhattan Resident Relief Coalition, an ad hoc alliance formed by Kwong Hui and Noah Rubin to meet the immediate needs of Lower Manhattan residents. This coalition helps residents bypass police barricades to make their medical appointments, distributes food, and advocates for social services for affected residents.

HARDSHIP &
SOLIDARITY

Workers at a temporary medical center in Manhattan treat firefighters
and policemen who suffered eye burns.

The Twin Towers once stood tall behind the statue of Lin Ze Xu in Lin Ze Xu Square in Chinatown. Now one can only see the American flag honoring the greatest heroes who fought for our freedom on Sept. 11, 2001.

Courtesy of Yujian Liu, *Coastide Magazine*

Courtesy of Asian American Federation of New York

A Chinese American man in New York's Chinatown wears a patriotic scarf, showing his loyalty to the U.S. Patriotism offers some comfort to those coming to terms with the horror of the attacks.

Muslim Americans, Sikh Americans....

CHAPTER **8**

CALL FOR TOLERANCE

Helen Zia speaks on racial intolerance and civil liberties after the September 11 attacks.

Every One of Us
By Helen Zia

"At least it's not Chinese this time." Those words, spoken by a fellow Chinese American, greeted me when I finally reached home on Sept. 15, 2001, after five harrowing days stranded in Washington, D.C., after the terrible events of September 11. I knew well enough the intended meaning of his remarks. After years of unrelenting innuendo that cast Chinese Americans and other Asian Americans as the evil invaders, "at least this time" some other group would play scapegoat. I suspect that many other Americans felt the same awkward relief that the terrorists were not "their kind." Even so, the words were painful to hear.

During those five days trapped in the confusion of the nation's capital, I spent much of that time in the hotel lobby watching the only television at the inn, which ordinarily brags that it has no TVs or radios in the guestrooms. I watched the horrifying news among strangers. With the exception of one other guest who, like me, had come to Washington to speak about Chinese Americans at a Smithsonian event scheduled on Sept. 11, 2001, everyone around us was white, European American.

I wept as I watched the dreadful images of the fallen Twin Towers, whose energy and bustle were part of my daily commute from New Jersey to Manhattan for years. Yet in this hotel lobby among these strangers, I felt that familiar stab of self-consciousness. Will the real American please stand up? In America, in this new millennium, an Asian face still signals "Foreigner"– especially at key patriotic moments.

September 11 was unquestionably one of those moments.

Washington in particular was well primed for xenophobia on the heels of the campaign finance probes, the bombing of the Chinese embassy in Belgrade, the persecution of Wen Ho Lee, and the spy plane showdown over China's Hainan Island. But I also knew that my own sense of racial vulnerability was nothing compared to the fear and distress of Middle Eastern, South Asian, Muslim, and Sikh Americans. Reports of violent assaults were already multiplying. I couldn't wait to leave the uncertainty of this emotionally delicate, partisan environment, to return to the comfort of family and friends.

During the plane ride home, I debated whether I should attend a community event scheduled for that evening, something I had promised many months ago. All I wanted to do was to go home, to find the illusion of a safe haven from the madness. But I also knew that Asian Americans could ill afford to be silent. I decided to go. When I arrived at the event, I ran into that acquaintance who gave me a conspiratorial look and said, "At least it's not Chinese Americans this time." His words made me feel ashamed to be one.

As a nation, our collective memory of shared history is so perishable, replaced instead by "instant" news, factoids, and MTV-like graphics that stimulate but don't educate. Asian Americans are no exception. "The Chinese seem to have a spy problem," was the word in some Asian American communities during the Wen Ho Lee case. "Campaign finance is not our problem," wrote a columnist in the JACL's *Pacific Citizen*. "What is it with the Koreans?" asked other Asian Americans during the rash of store boycotts. "It's not my ox that's being gored," an African American feminist colleague said to me after Jimmy Breslin's racist and sexist tirade against a Korean American woman journalist. "Me not Japanese" was the sad little window sign scrawled by a Chinese American shopkeeper during World War II, a sentiment shared at the time by some Korean Americans who wore buttons declaring, "I hate J-ps more than you do."

There is no escaping the fragility of cross-group unity at times of crisis. Yet there are reasons for optimism as well. While I was stuck in Washington, I had the privilege of attending a hastily called meeting of concerned Asian Americans- most of whom were civil servants or representatives of Asian American advocacy groups in DC. The meeting was held at SEARAC, the Southeast Asian Resource Action Center, and among the organizers were several South Asian Americans, including Sikh Americans. The meeting's chair was an Indian American woman.

Only two days after 9/11, these organizers pulled together an impressive pan-Asian coalition to plan a national candlelight vigil at the Japanese American National Memorial on the mall. Their purpose was to draw attention to the need for tolerance and restraint in the face of hate crimes and domestic terrorism against Arab, Muslims and South Asian Americans. Their inspiring efforts in the midst of national crisis succeeded in garnering the attention of the media, other civil rights groups, members of Congress, and even the White House.

This example stands in sharp contrast to those Asian Americans who might find solace in the false notion that yellow Americans won't be racially profiled. These folks must not have noticed how the news blared "SECOND PEARL HARBOR," while at the same time failed to mention the architect who designed the World Trade Center. The acclaimed Minoru Yamasaki, a second-generation Japanese American, had designed the World Trade Center as his crowning glory, dedicated to peace-as just about every website on the towers prominently recounted. Regarding this omission, I am certain of two points: first, every newsroom possessed the information that Yamasaki designed the fallen skyscrapers. Second, a conscious decision was made in each newsroom to not mention this "minor" detail, lest the Asianness of the World Trade Center's creator detract from the theme of an America under kamikaze attack.

There were plenty of topics I had intended to bring up at the Smithsonian panel on Chinese Americans: the spy plane incident over China and the anti-Chinese, anti-Asian racism that followed. Talk show hosts called for the internment of Chinese Americans and made live, on-air "ching chong" calls to people with Chinese surnames, picked at random from phone books. Members of the American Society of Newspaper Editors, the top editors of the nation's newspapers who are supposedly dedicated to "objectivity" in the news, hooted and howled at a performance featuring white actors in yellow-face, pretending to be Chinese. The ASNE refused to acknowledge their biases even after one of their employees, a Chinese American student intern, called them on their racism.

Even before the spy plane incident, the Committee of 100 had conducted its landmark survey on American attitudes toward Chinese and Asian Americans. The results included these points:
• 34% of those polled believe Chinese Americans are more loyal to the People's Republic of China than to their country, the United States of America.

CALL FOR TOLERANCE

Muslim Americans, Sikh Americans, and South Asian Americans were subjected to harassment and violence immediately following the September 11 attacks. Concerned residents and communities expressed their views on the ongoing crisis of war in the Middle East and of civil liberties in the U.S. They participated in silent marches for peace and unity.

CALL FOR TOLERANCE

- 32% believe that Chinese Americans have too much influence on high technology
- 42% believe that Chinese Americans are likely to pass U.S. secrets to China.
- 68% feel negative about Chinese Americans and Asian Americans.

The poll had asked two separate samples of Americans the same questions. One group was asked about Chinese Americans and the other about Asian Americans. There was no statistical difference in responses by the two samples. So here was hard evidence of the "racial lumping" that is so well known to every Asian American kid who was ever called the slur of another Asian ethnicity.

Then there was the former Los Alamos nuclear scientist Wen Ho Lee. The book I co-authored with Dr. Lee, *My Country Versus Me*, details how he was racially profiled by the U.S. government in the name of national security. When the FBI couldn't find any evidence of spying, they charged him instead with 59 counts of "mishandling of classified information." No one had ever been so charged before, even though many others had mishandled classified information, including John Deutch, the former CIA director. Deutch received mere a slap on the wrist, and then a Clinton Presidential pardon. Wen Ho Lee was imprisoned nine months in solitary confinement, where he was chained and manacled in "pretrial detention." He was finally released, with an apology from the federal judge. Yet there are reports of other Asian American scientists and technical workers who have also been racially profiled.

Of course, the Smithsonian event never took place on that September 11, 2001. But the racial profiling against "Middle Eastern appearing people" followed with a vengeance—more than 700 reported hate incidents in only a few weeks, with several deaths. Among them were South Asian Americans, particularly those of the Sikh faith. To the list of those killed by international terrorists,

we now have a growing list of those killed in hate crimes by domestic terrorists.

Shortly after 9/11, White House and National Security Advisor Condoleeza Rice warned the nation's news executives against publishing or broadcasting "propaganda" from the enemy, including possibly "coded messages" from Osama bin Laden. Within hours, network executives promised more judicious "editing" [read: self-censorship] in the future.

This bit about "coded messages" from Osama bin Laden reminded me of the accusations made against Los Alamos scientist Wen Ho Lee. The FBI had argued that Dr. Lee's mere "hello" might contain a secret message for agents from China—messages that could result in the production of an advanced nuclear warhead. The FBI warned that Ninja warriors from China might arrive in black helicopters at the mountaintop laboratories of Los Alamos to spirit Wen Ho Lee away. Never mind that Ninjas are Japanese warriors, not Chinese, or that it would be very tough for enemy aircraft of any kind to go unnoticed in the secluded and heavily guarded laboratory town.

This was the same FBI whose intelligence failed to detect any clues of the September 11 attacks, and which now has unbridled policing powers, thanks to the Patriot Act, which allows the FBI and law enforcement to imprison suspects indefinitely without charging any crime or immigration violation. It also provides no meaningful opportunity for a hearing to determine the reason for an individual's detention. All details of arrests and detention are secret, sealed under court order. All in the name of national security. Of course, "threat to national security" was the same justification used to shackle Wen Ho Lee and to incarcerate 120,000 Japanese Americans during World War II.

In the 1940s, newspapers ran headlines about Japanese American farmers who could grow tomatoes that would point to U.S. airbases, so that a field of tomatoes could guide enemy pilots to their targets. The esteemed Edward R. Murrow, patron saint of American journalism, announced on his radio broadcasts that any Japanese fighter pilots who made it to Seattle would surely be wearing University of Washington sweaters. None of this was true, but people believed what was repeated in the news media.

All Americans should be concerned about and actively watchful over the media's power. Asian Americans know this lesson well. Those rare moments in our history when we rose from media invisibility, we were used as a hammer, a wedge, toward someone else's divisive agenda. We've been the "heathen Chinee," the "hordes of hungry Hindoos," and the countless string of other hateful names that raised the ire of white workers; we've also been labeled the "model minority" to divert the civil rights movement and bring down affirmative action. Asian Americans have been played as the bystander and the weapon. Indeed, the miracle of modern media was the overnight conversion of Asian Americans from the Evil Enemy Within to the Modern American Success Story.

Today, we find news stories of yellow Asian Americans attacking brown Asian Americans-sick players in this patriotic zealotry, weird mutants of equal opportunity hate. This is not the time for any Asian Americans to breathe easy and sigh, "At least it's not us, this time." It is us, every one of us. If Americans of every color and religion aren't speaking out against these travesties, then we are part of the problem, collaborators in our own oppressions.

Not long after September 11, I drove down to San Diego from San Francisco with my life partner, Lia. We didn't want to fly-not because we were fearful, but to avoid the airport camouflage uniforms, the automatic weapons, the searches and the reminders of the military state we are rapidly becoming. Near San Diego, I pulled into a gas station. The entire shift was immigrant labor-Latinos,

Arabs, East Asian. The young Latino cashier shoved a plastic license plate flag into my face. It was decorated with a painted American flag. "You should buy this, only $3.95." I muttered a no thank you, and he tried again, "Don't you love the flag?" This time I said, "I wear the flag in my heart, not on my car." He tried again. "You can show you are American." I thought of my immigrant parents and felt sad for all the immigrants who are now so compelled to have the most prominent American flags. I took my change and said, "I am American. You are too. Even without a flag."

I actually do have an American flag, made of heavy canvas. It's folded in a neat triangle. The last time it was unfurled, it decorated the coffin of a laundry worker and a World War II veteran, David Bing Hing Chin—the father of Vincent Chin. He died six months before Vincent was beaten to death by two white autoworkers in 1982. His mother, Lily Chin, gave the flag to me when she moved to China, after spending 40 of her 60 years in the U.S., as a naturalized American. She left her home here because it was too painful to be reminded that her son was killed out of hate, struck down like an animal, and then discarded by a justice system that didn't believe an Asian American could be the target of racism. She gave the flag to me because she didn't want it anymore.

For almost 15 years now, I have kept this flag in a safe place. I took it out a few weeks after September 11. Not out of sentimentality, I confess, but because a professor asked me to find a document related to Vincent Chin's case. When I searched through my files, there was the flag. Its colors were as vibrant and strong as ever. The indigo blue. The deep blood red. As I held the canvas triangle of red, white, and blue, I gave silent remembrance to Vincent and David Bing Hing Chin. Other names came upon me as well, those of the new victims of domestic terrorism, new names and stories keep popping up in my email–Adel Karas, an Arab American; Balbir Singh Sodhi and Surjit Samra, both

CALL FOR TOLERANCE

South Asian, Sikh Americans; and so many others. I remembered those who died in the World Trade Center, the Pentagon, and the hijacked planes. I hugged the flag and remembered that this country was founded in defense of liberty, against tyranny. This is also what it means to be American.

I hope Asian Americans will use our special experiences in this nation's history to speak up, as Americans, to offer some light on these dark topics. We have much experience to share that will strengthen this nation. I hope all Americans will remember the words of the Rev. Dr. Martin Luther King: "Darkness cannot put out darkness. Only light can do that."

Helen Zia is the author of *Asian American Dreams: The Emergence of an American People* (Farrar Straus & Giroux, 2000), and co-author of *My Country Versus Me*, the story of Dr. Wen Ho Lee (Hyperion, 2002). The original version of this article was first published in UCLA's journal *On War and Peace* in *spring* 2002. Copyright © 2003-2004 by Helen Zia. Adapted from her essay, "Oh Say, Can You See?" Reprinted with permission.

Zehra Naqvi speaks about the public attention she received as a result of her South Asian American and Muslim American identity. Naqvi is a member of a South Asian American poets group in Washington, D.C.

Visibility

By Zehra Naqvi

I used to wonder if invisibility was the curse of my color
But visibility has brought me nothing but anger
This tan color has made me a target for hate
Bulls-eyed as the consequence of one day's fate

I'd rather be invisible than accused of things I didn't do
I'd rather be the girl from who-knows-where than one of
the you-know-whos
I prayed for days I would not have to pinpoint my
origins on a map
But today I am just one of those people that wear
those funny head-wraps

Today, people know where I'm from and instead ask
where I'm headed
My holy book, my beliefs, and my look are now
dreaded
I wonder if I wished too hard for recognition and
visibility
But it's too late now to redefine those boundaries

I've got misconceptions to correct and words to get out
If I can't be invisible, I might as well shout
I'm wishing for recognition for who I truly am
Not just the things that ignorant stereotypes demand

The only Jihad I practice is to educate and empower
Minds and hearts to look beyond religion and color
And instead of waiting for civilizations to war
I'm going to try to get us all to learn from before

History is screaming for our ears to hear
That violence "over there" just brings it here
That hate against "them" brings hate against us
Let lessons from the past be our compass

If we are divided, then we are conquered
It is by this moment that we will be measured
By history, by generations, by our conscience
Did we seek to learn the truth or bow to vengeance?

Villains commit harm out of blind rage
Is this the same war that we are about to wage
Against our own, against what we know to be right
Will our dead be brought back by a show of might?

I did not ask to be made visible by the light of
explosions
And I refuse to be defined by others' mistaken notions
I will not let visibility overwhelm me
I pledge to use it to help others be seen

Grandma Wears Red, White and Blue
By Dana Nakano

She and I have never talked much
beyond the how are you,
I haven't seen you in a while.

She asked me to show her
how to change the channel with the remote.
I did so, willingly.
Silently.

My grandmother.
Nisei woman.
Quiet American.
She said nothing,
but I noticed.

I noticed the flag on her purse
and it wasn't the fourth of July.

Post 9/11,
fallen twin towers
bring memories of
a bombed harbor and pointed fingers
in a not-so-distant past.

It wasn't until months after that fateful morning
when I believed that my family was lucky and
unaffected
that I noticed.

I noticed Grandma wearing
red, white and blue.

With stars and stripes draped across her sweatshirt,
she knitted the colors of the American flag into her
afghan.

Make no mistake, she is an American.
This blanket, this t-shirt,
these key chains, that bumper sticker, must prove it;
because nothing else seems to be enough.

She knows all too well
her birth,
her citizenship,
her only knowing the life and ways of this country
mean nothing
when wrapped in yellow.

Grandma wears red, white and blue.
A flag on her sweater, a pin on her jacket,
a ring on her finger
hoping, maybe
it will all cover up
any other color they might see in her.

This time
there is no round up at the racetrack,
train trip to the swamps of Arkansas,
three years behind barbed wire
under the guise of
'keeping her safe from hysteria'.
Insincerity's rifles, pointed inward,
aim squarely at her abandoned heart.

Success.

But I want to tell her.
I want to let her know
these colors shield her from nothing.
These colors don't cover the yellow of her skin.

She's safe today
because no one is looking for her.

But maybe
that was never her purpose.
Maybe her scheme was
not to prove anything.

Maybe Grandma wears red, white and blue
because she is an American
and proud.

Because her birth,
her citizenship,
her only knowing
the life and ways of this country
mean something to her.

She wears red, white and blue
not because she has to,
not to save herself,
but because she can.
Because it's her choice to make.
Her choice.

It's not for me to say.
I don't know.
Because I want to know,
but I can't find the question,
the moment.

She and I have never talked much
beyond the how are you.

Courtesy of Emmy Akiyama

Dana Nakano expresses his feelings
about his grandmother's American
loyalty through his spoken-word lyrics.

Hate Through My Eyes
By Tara Kaur Dhingra

No one thought it was possible
No one imagined it could happen
The day the unthinkable came true
Was 9-11.
Thousands of innocent lives claimed
Children without parents
Suddenly the fingers were pointing
And chaos soon struck.
Shootings, beatings and harassment
The hate crimes have begun.
Hate, was the cause of 9-11 and
Hate, was the effect.

Anyone with a turban
Was automatically a suspect.
This can't be right
Something must be done.
Everyone is acting out of fear
And not bothering to learn
What kind of life is this?
This is not the way

Ignorance is fear; fear is hate
Hate kills, it must be stopped

Let us all unite and
Protect our freedom.

Terrorists tried to take it away
Will we let them succeed?
Let us stop the hate crimes

And gather in peace.

My father wears his turban
With pride and grace
He is not a Muslim
He is an American Sikh.
We may be a minority
But does that give you the right
To take away our freedom
And make us feel small?

I was called a terrorist, and
I was told to go home
The truth is
This is my home.

I am an American
Proud and strong
And I am here to stay.

Courtesy of Sikh Mediawatch and Resource Task Force

Mansheel Singh Rajpal, age 17, is proud of his Sikh American identity: his turban and beard.

My Turban
By Mansheel Singh Rajpal

Every day is a struggle for me. Things have only gotten worse since 9/11. There's not a day I don't get called "Osama bin Laden" or "diaper head." They declare me a terrorist because of my appearance. I have to constantly watch my back and minimize exposing myself. Most days I don't eat lunch outside to avoid the racist calls across campus. Both the students and teachers have given me racist threats and remarks. On one occasion, a teacher at my high school grabbed my beard, pulled it, and said that I was a member of the Taliban. When they call me these names and threaten me, my faith only becomes stronger. As far as I'm concerned, if my people have been giving their lives for centuries to keep their identity, then I have nothing to complain about. My turban is my crown and my beard is my mane.

The Asians United to Raise Awareness (AURA) Fund holds the charity concert "My America" to commemorate the losses and the heroism of Asian Americans and Pacific Islanders during the events of September 11, and to raise awareness of issues facing these communities in its aftermath. Bringing together Asian American and Pacific Islander musical performers from different genres—rock to jazz, pop to Broadway—the concert presents new ways to think about America and what it represents to Asian Americans and Pacific Islanders and the rest of the world.

CALL FOR TOLERANCE

Below is a song titled "My America" written by Jeff Yang and Kevin So for a September 11 memorial concert sponsored by Asians United to Raise Awareness(AURA).

MY AMERICA
Music by Kevin So; Lyrics by Jeff Yang/Kevin So
Copyright: 2002, Kevin So and Jeff Yang.
All Rights Reserved.

[VERSE 1]
We sailed across the water
We soared across the sky
Walked across the Western border
With our hearts and hopes held high
My father and his father
My mother and her child
Sought a place where they could live
Beyond the ocean wild

[CHORUS]
We went in search of my America
Left home to find my America
Dreamed a dream of my America
We came and made it our America
We planted seeds in my America
Raised the flag of my America
Stood our ground in my America
We came and made it our America

[VERSE 2]
Among the soaring mountains
Along the sparkling sands
We placed our mark upon the soil
We worked it with our hands
We built this nation's railroads
We fed and clothed it too
Marched in peace and died in honor
Somehow we made it through

[CHORUS]
We went in search of my America
Left home to find my America
Dreamed a dream of my America
We came and made it our America
We planted seeds in my America
Raised the flag of my America
Stood our ground in my America
We came and made it our America

[BRIDGE/ENDING]
My country 'tis of thee
Celebrate our legacy
Weave us in your tapestry
Write a page in your history

This is our history
This is our America
Sweet land of liberty
This is My America

CALL FOR TOLERANCE

On Sept. 22, 2001, in Jackson Heights, Queens, home to a large South Asian American community, more than 150 residents participate in a silent march for peace and a candlelight vigil. Among those marching are representatives from Workers' AWAAZ, a non-profit organization that organizes South Asian American domestic workers. The march proceeds to the 74th Street subway station where speakers rally for peace. Among those speaking is State Senator Satveer Chaudhary from Minnesota.

116

Deepa Iyer, board member of South Asian American Leaders for Tomorrow (SAALT), is interviewed by the media, one week after September 11, at the Japanese American memorial in Washington, D.C.. At the press conference, SAALT and other national Asian American and Pacific Islander organizations call for unity after media reports that South Asian Americans and Sikh and Muslim Americans were being targeted.

Courtesy of Daphne Kwok

Courtesy of J.K. Yamamoto, *Hokubei Mainichi Newspaper*

Japanese peace activists take part in an anti-war rally marching on Market Street in San Francisco.

CALL FOR TOLERANCE

Students protest against random attacks on
Muslims and the invasion of Afghanistan.

A woman prays at a peace rally in Union
Square, New York, Sept. 22, 2001.

Banners in Union Square call for "Peace for Humanity"
on the night of Sept. 17, 2001.

To promote peace, college student
Saori Shibata teaches interested
children and adults how to fold
origami paper cranes, an international
symbol of peace. She did this for
three consecutive days in Union
Square Park, Manhattan.

An exhibit entitled "Below the Canal: After 9/11"....

CHAPTER 9
ART FOR PEACE

"September 11th Memorial Installation" Mixed Media With Audio

By Chee Wang Ng

The September 11 tragedy brought out great, massive expressions of grieving in all levels of society, from silent, private cries to huge public vigils. I had to break my own code to speak out on this defiance to humanity. To heal this raw pain and anger is the only way that I know how. This installation is my personal offering to September 11 and the loss of the World Trade Center Twin Towers. It cries for the nation's loss of her innocent, transforming the seven red stripes of the U.S. flag into the seven red bleeding lines – the blood of the victims wrap around the large bowl. The 10-inch-diameter bowl is filled with rice not for the living but as a sacrificial offering to the dead. The chopsticks mark the Chinese taboo of sticking vertically into the rice bowl, ghostly resembling the lost World Trade Center Twin Towers. Encircling the bowl are the 50 stars of the 50 states, on the blue prayer candles shimmering and longing for the departed. This is a round, low table for one. When will world nations join in and share at this table of humanity?

This installation was featured at the Asian American Arts Centre exhibition entitled, "In the Shadow of 9/11: A Chinatown Memorial Exhibition," held September through October 2003 in New York City, and at the Savannah College of Art and Design exhibition entitled, "In Response," held Sept. 4 through Nov. 5, 2002, in Savannah, Georgia.

"September 11th Memorial Installation" Courtesy of Chee Wang Ng

ART FOR PEACE

An exhibit entitled "Below the Canal: After 9/11" opened at the Asian American Arts Centre located on Bowery Street in Chinatown, New York City on March 21, 2003. The Centre, a non-profit organization, was founded in 1974 to present both traditional and contemporary art and culture to Asian American and Pacific Islander communities and the general public. By gathering diverse artists in Lower Manhattan, including Chinatown, this exhibit was designed to revitalize New York City. Among the artists featured were Paul K. Wong, Choong Sup Lim, and Naoto Nakagawa, whose works were directly inspired by the September 11 tragedy.

BELOW THE CANAL AFTER

CANAL ST

Grimanesa Amoros · Olivia Beens · Tis
Jane Freeman · Carter Hodgkin · Choong
A. Lebowski · Pamela Lee · Choong
Karen Margolis · John
Naoto Nakagawa · Pao
Richard Rudich · Pau
www.artspiral.org

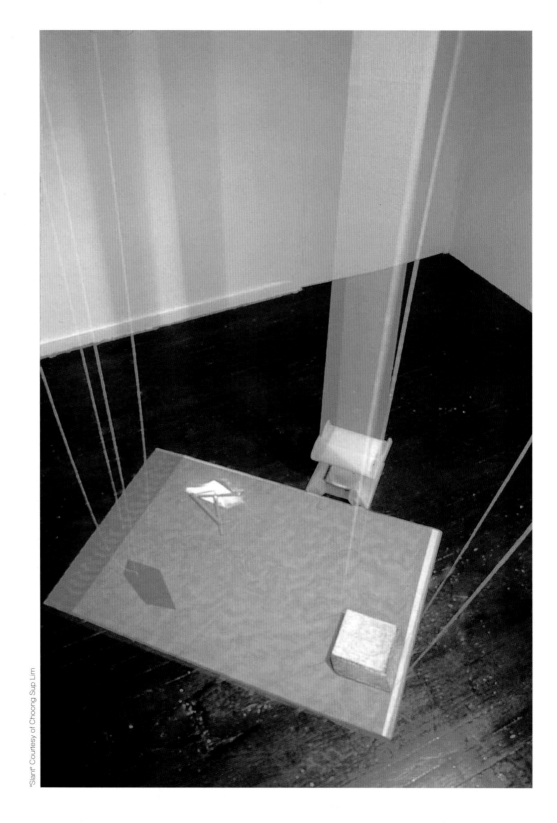

"Slant" Courtesy of Choong Sup Lim

122

"Slant"

By Choong Sup Lim

I was home in my Tribeca studio when the planes hit the World Trade Center. I opened my window and my neighbor was shouting. The attack was an eerie reminder of growing up in the "war generation"–the civil war in Korea.

"Slant" for me implies a gesture toward a realigning. "Slant" is an instinct to go back to the original situation where it began. In Asia, the meaning of cotton thread is not only its practical usage in that it ties two different parts together by sewing; it is also a symbol of spiritual purity and humble character. Negative space speaks to the space around positive space, well known in traditional Asian landscape paintings. By utilizing space with acute consciousness, I want nothingness to become pregnant with the meaning of emptiness as wholeness.

On 9/11/2001, the unexpected attacks not only struck the World Trade Center Towers, they also struck "verticality" as conceived in Western culture. Verticality is an aspect of Western architectural concepts. This tragic incident offers my work an opportunity to awaken the possibility of reconciling the Western concept of verticality and the Eastern ideal of negative space by means of a single cotton thread.

Mediation in this context is like being "Slant." Buddha never stands on any extreme pole to love humans. He always stands between the horizontal and the vertical to exemplify the middle path. It took me a year and a half to create this installation.

"Bamiyan"
By Paul K. Wong

After witnessing the attack and destruction of the World Trade Center Towers, I, among other artists living in Tribeca, could not return to making art for months afterwards. I was paralyzed by the simplicity of doing artwork in comparison to such a horrifying event. This piece, "Bamiyan," refers to another destructive event executed by the Taliban in March 2001 in the ancient Afghani region of Gandhara, northwest of Kabul. Between the second and fifth centuries A.D., two colossal Buddhas standing 115 and 175 feet tall were carved into sandstone cliffs, surrounded by scores of cave sanctuaries where pilgrims visiting the site found refuge. These two monuments were shelled and detonated with explosives to proclaim Taliban Sunni Muslim extremism toward grand images and to decimate national symbols. I have photocopied before and after images of the major Bamiyan Buddha and transformed them onto paper infused with vermillion Chinese joss paper to address the destruction of such historic artifacts due to intolerance bred by opposing cultural and religious differences so volatile now.

ART FOR PEACE

"Stars of the Forest Elegy"
By Naoto Nakagawa

The morning of 9/11, I was mixing paints for the day's work as I've been doing every morning for the past 24 years. When my Tribeca studio shook for a second, I thought it was an earth tremor. A few minutes later, my wife Caroline called me to tell me that there had been a terrible accident at the World Trade Center. In the early 1970s from my Chamber Street studio, I had watched the World Trade Center go up. I felt in awe of its scale and height and also regret that so many beautiful buildings and old shops–part of New York City's unique landscape–had to be destroyed to make way for those towers. I have witnessed the tallest building in New York City go up and fall down, destroyed along with so many lives.

This picture was painted after 9/11. At the time, I was unaware that it would be an elegy for that disaster. In fact, the image had been in my mind for almost a year, inspired by some beautiful star-shaped moss I had seen on a forest floor. It shone in the morning dew, the sunlight glinting and giving it vivid colors, like blue nesting in yellow, orange, and flaming red. It was a glorious moment in nature's drama. I wanted to capture it in print! As I was completing the painting, after working on it for three months, I came to realize what it was about. The inner light that permeates the entire surface represents all the victims of 9/11, each expressed as a shining star.

ART FOR
PEACE

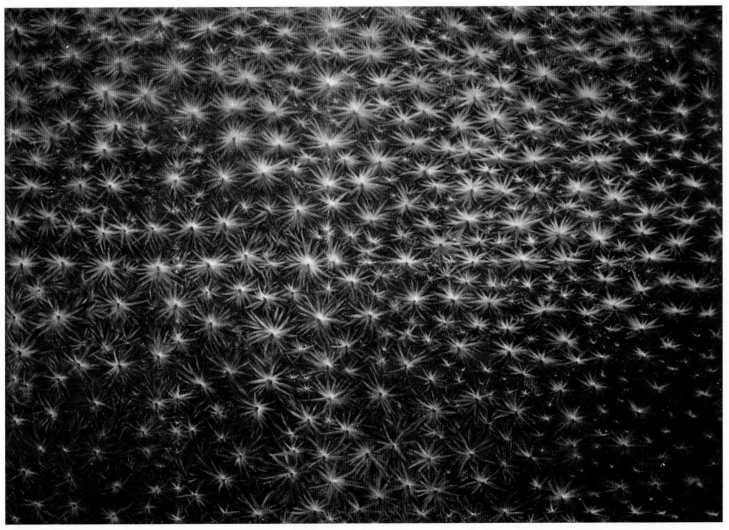

"Stars of the Forest Elegy" Courtesy of Naoto Nakagawa

Children around the country expressed....

Located near the World Trade Center, New York's Chinatown community was directly and significantly affected by the events of September 11. Many residents, especially children, felt confused, alone, and vulnerable. In response, CORE (Children Overcoming through Resources and Education), a post-September 11 mental health initiative, was developed by the Coalition for Asian American Children and Families (CACF) to help Chinatown children and families cope and heal as a community. Project CORE provides events and education programs for the community, and training for mental health professionals and after-school providers who help children and their families re-establish connections with their community. The CACF is a non-profit organization dedicated to improving the health and well-being of Asian American and Pacific Islander children in New York City.

The following poems, authored by Alan Cheng, Emmily Hu, and Erica Leung, as well as the drawing by Justin Zhang, are part of the CORE project.

Emmily Hu,
age 10, writes in her poem that she feels safe with
her mother in the devastated streets.

Still Standing

America was attacked
People cried when the towers collapsed.
Our landscape is destroyed
But in our hearts,
There will always be the Twin Towers.

Walking down the street
Dark and scary
I get closer to my mom
no longer afraid.

America was attacked
we will always fight back,
me and my friend Erica
said God bless America.

Erica Leung,
age 10, writes in her poem that the Twin Towers
will always be in her heart.

Memories of the Twin Towers

It stood tall there,

perfectly

its view was perfect

Showing its proudly made antenna

from the distance

lighting up

it's not there anymore now,

but it's still here in my heart.

My memories of it will never fade.

YOUNG VOICES

Children around the country expressed their feelings of fear, anger, remembrance, and love through drawings and words shortly after the September 11 terrorist attacks. Some chronicled the horror they experienced on that fateful day while others expressed their gratitude and respect for all the heroes and rescue workers who brought solace to the families of the missing.

Justin Zhang,
age 10, draws a New York City firefighter with the stars and stripes as his reflection on September 11.

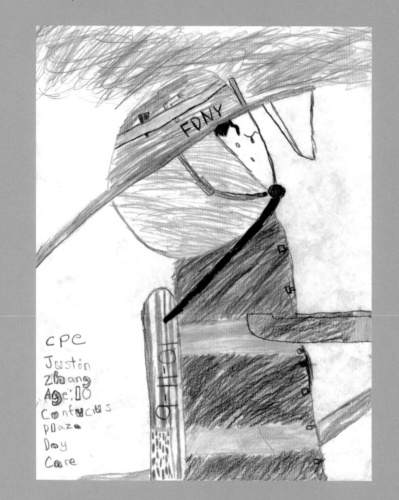

Alan Cheng,
age 9, writes in his poem that he feels safe once he sees his home.

The Door To My Home

Once I see
The door to my home
I know that
I'll be safe.
I won't be
Harmed at
All.
I will be
With my
family.

Courtesy of South Asian Youth Action

September 11 had a devastating impact on the lives of South Asian youth and their families. Many found themselves subjected to violence, employment and housing discrimination, and racial profiling. Many were faced with issues of cultural identity and fearful for their future in America. The South Asian Youth Action (SAYA) in New York City launched the post 9-11 Peace and Unity Initiative to address the new needs of the South Asian youth, and to build positive relationships with other community youth organizations. The mural shown here, painted by SAYA youth, promotes greater peace and unity among young people of diverse racial, ethnic and religious backgrounds.

REMEMBRANCE

Kathleen A. Burns , Kathleen Hunt Casey , Kathleen Moran , Kathleen Nicosia , Kathryn Anne, Shatzoff , Kathryn Blair Lee , Kathryn L. ... ... Marie McCloskey , Katsuyuki Hirai , Kazuhiro Anai , Kazushige Ito , Keiichiro Takahashi , Keiji Takahashi , Keith Alexander Glascoe , Keith Broomfi... ...rns , Keith K. O'Connor , Keith McHeffey , Keith Roma , Keithroy Maynard , Kelly Ann Booms , Kenichiro Tanaka , Kenneth Alan Simon , Kenneth ... ...nneth F. Tietjen , Kenneth Grouzalis , Kenneth J. Swensen , Kenneth John Cubas , Kenneth Joseph Marino , Kenneth Joseph Tarantino , Kennet... ...arcus Caldwell , Kenneth P. Lira , Kenneth W. Van Auken , Kenneth W. White , Kenneth Waldie , Kenneth Watson , Kenneth William Basnicki , Kere... ...ennis , Kevin Francis Cleary , Kevin Francis Conroy , Kevin H. Bracken , Kevin James Hannaford , Kevin James Murphy , Kevin Joseph Frawley , Kevin L. Dowl... ...Kevin Michael Williams , Kevin Nathaniel Colbert , Kevin O. Reilly , Kevin O'Rourke , Kevin P. Connors , Kevin Patrick York , Kevin Prior , Kevin Raymond Crotty , Kevin Sanford Cohen , Kevin Smith , Kevin T. Szocik , Kevin Wayne Yokum , Khalid M. Shahid , Khamladai K. (Khami) Singh , Khang Nguyen , Kieran Gorman , Kimberly S. Bowers , Kiran Reddy Gopu , Kirsten L. Christophe , Kirsten Santiago , Klaus Bothe , Klaus Johannes Sprockamp , Kleber Rolando Molina , Kris R. Hughes , Kris Romeo Bishundat , Krishna Moorthy , Kristen Fiedel , Kristen Montanaro , Kristin A. Irvine Ryan , Kristine M. Swearson , Krystine C. Bordenabe , Kui Fai Kwok , Kum-Kum Girolamo , Kyung (Kaccy) Cho , Lance Richard Tumulty , Larry Bowman , Larry I. Beck , Larry John Senko , Lars Peter Qualben , LaShawana Johnson , Laura A. Giglio , Laura Angilletta , Laura Gilly , Laura Lee Morabito , Laura M. Longing , Laura Marie Ragonese-Snik , Laura Rockefeller , Lauren Grandcolas , Laurence Christopher Abel , Laurence Curia , Laurence M. Polatsch , Laurence Nedell , Laurie Ann Neira , Lawrence Davidson , Lawrence Don Kim , Lawrence Francis Boisseau , Lawrence Patrick Dickinson , Lawrence T. Stack , Lawrence Veling , Lawrence Virgilio , Leah E. Oliver , Leanne Marie Whiteside , Lee Adler , Lee Charles Ludwig , Lee S. Fehling , Leo A. Roberts , Leo Russell Keene , Leobardo Lopez Pascual , Leon Lebor , Leon Smith , Leonard Anthony White , Leonard J. Snyder , Leonard M. Castrianno , Leonard Ragaglia , Leonard Taylor , Leonard William Hatton , Leonel Morocho , Leroy Homer , Lesley Anne Thomas , Leslie A. Whittington , Lester Vincent Marino , Liam Callahan , Liam Joseph Colhoun , Lillian Caceres , Lillian I. Frederick , Liming (Michael) Gu , Lincoln Quappe , Linda C. Lee , Linda George , Linda Gronlund , Linda Jones , Linda Luzzicone , Linda M. Colon , Linda Mair Grayling , Linda Mary Oliva , Linda Rivera , Linda Rosenbaum , Linda Sheehan , Lindsay Coates Herkness , Lindsay S. Morehouse , Lisa B. Cannava , Lisa Caren Weinstein Ehrlich , Lisa Egan , Lisa Fenn Gordenstein , Lisa Frost , Lisa J. Raines , Lisa Kearney-Griffin , Lisa L. Trerotola , Lisa L. Young , Lisa M. King-Johnson , Lisa Marie Terry , Lizette Mendoza , Lizie Martinez-Calderon , Lloyd Brown , Lloyd D. Rosenberg , Lonny J. Stone , Lorenzo Ramzey , Loretta A Vero , Lorisa Ceylon Taylor , Lorraine D. Antigua , Lorraine G. Bay , Lorraine Lee , Lorraine Lisi , Louie Anthony Williams , Louis A. Caporicci , Louis Arena , Louis Calvin Williams , Louis F. Aversano Jr , Louis J. Nacke , Louis Joseph Minervino , Louis Neil Mariani , Louis S. Inghilterra , Louis V. Fersini , Louise A. Lynch , Lourdes Galletti Diaz , Lt. Andrew Desperito , Lt. Anthony Jovic , Lt. Brian G. Ahearn , Lt. Charles Joseph Margiotta , Lt. Charles William Garbarini , Lt. Christopher P. Sullivan , Lt. Cmdr. David Lucian Williams , Lt. Cmdr. Eric Allen Cranford , Lt. Cmdr. Otis Vincent Tolbert , Lt. Cmdr. Patrick Jude Murphy , Lt. Cmdr. Robert Randolph Elseth , Lt. Cmdr. Ronald James Vauk , Lt. Col. Canfield D. Boone , Lt. Col. David M. Scales , Lt. Col. Dean E. Mattson , Lt. Col. Dennis M. Johnson , Lt. Col. Jerry Don Dickerson , Lt. Col. Karen Wagner , Lt. Col. Stephen Neil Hyland , Lt. Daniel O'Callaghan , Lt. Dennis Mojica , Lt. Edward Alexander D'Atri , Lt. Gen. Timothy J. Maude , Lt. Glenn C. Perry , Lt. Glenn Wilkinson , Lt. Gregg Arthur Atlas , Lt. Harvey L. Harrell , Lt. J.G. Darin Howard Pontell , Lt. John Crisci , Lt. John F. Ginley , Lt. John R. Fischer , Lt. John Williamson , Lt. Jonas Martin Panik , Lt. Joseph Gerard Leavey , Lt. Joseph Gullickson , Lt. Kenneth John Phelan , Lt. Kevin Christopher Dowdell , Lt. Kevin Pfeifer , Lt. Kevin W. Donnelly , Lt. Michael Esposito , Lt. Michael K. Healey , Lt. Michael N. Fodor , Lt. Michael Quilty , Lt. Michael Scott Lamana , Lt. Michael Thomas Russo , Lt. Michael Warchola , Lt. Paul Richard Martini , Lt. Paul Thomas Mitchell , Lt. Peter L. Freund , Lt. Peter Martin , Lt. Philip S. Petti , Lt. Raymond E. Murphy , Lt. Robert B. Nagel , Lt. Robert Dominick Cirri , Lt. Robert F. Wallace , Lt. Robert M. Regan , Lt. Ronald T. Kerwin , Lt. Stephen Gary Harrell , Lt. Steven J. Bates , Lt. Thomas O'Hagan , Lt. Timothy Higgins , Lt. Vernon Allan Richard , Lt. Vincent Francis Giammona , Lt. Vincent Gerard Halloran , Lt. William E. McGinn , Lucia Crifasi , Lucille T. King , Lucy Fishman , Ludwig John Picarro , Luigi Calvi , Luis Alfonso Chimbo , Luis Clodoaldo Revilla Mier , Luis Eduardo Torres , Luis Jimenez , Luis Lopez , Luis Morales , Lukas (Luke) Rambousek , Lukasz T. Milewski , Luke A. Dudek , Luke G. Nee , Lydia Estelle Bravo , Lynette D. Vosges , Lynn Angell , Lynn Catherine Goodchild , Lynne Irene Morris , Lyudmila Ksido , Maclovio Lopez Jr. , Madeline Sweeney , Maile Rachel Hale , Maj. Clifford L. Patterson , Maj. Dwayne Williams , Maj. Kip P. Taylor , Maj. Ronald D. Milam , Maj. Steve Long , Maj. Wallace Cole Hogan , Malissa White , Mandy Chang , Manette Marie Beckles , Manika Narula , Manish K. Patel , Mannie Leroy Clark , Manuel Da Mota , Manuel Dejesus Molina , Manuel Del Valle , Manuel Emilio Mejia , Manuel Gomez , Manuel L. Lopez , Manuel Mojica , Manuel O. Asitimbay , Manuel Patrocino , Marc A. Murolo , Marc Scott Zeplin , Marcello Matricciano , Marcia G. Cecil-Carter , Marcia Hoffman , Marco Motroni , Marcus R. Neblett , Margaret Ann (Peggy) Jezycki Alario , Margaret Elaine Mattic , Margaret L. Benson , Margaret Mary Conner , Margaret Orloske , Margaret Ruth Echtermann , Margaret Seeliger , Margaret Susan Lewis , Margarito Casillas , Maria Behr , Maria Isabel Ramirez , Maria Jakubiak , Maria Lavache , Maria Percoco Vola , Maria Rose Abad , Maria Theresa Santillan , Marian Hrycak , Marian Serva , Marianne MacFarlane , Marianne Simone , Marie Lukas , Marie Pappalardo , Marina R. Gertsberg , Mario L. Santoro , Mario Nardone , Marion Britton , Marion Victoria (vickie) Manning , Mari-Rae Sopper , Marisa Di Nardo Schorpp , Marjorie C. Salamone , Mark A. Brisman , Mark Bavis , Mark Bruce , Mark D. Hindy , Mark E. Schurmeier , Mark F. Hemschoot , Mark Francis Broderick , Mark G. Ludvigsen , Mark H. Rosen , Mark J. Colaio , Mark J. Ellis , Mark Jardim , Mark K. Bingham , Mark L. Charette , Mark Louis Rosenberg , Mark Petrocelli , Mark Rothenberg , Mark Ryan McGinly , Mark Schwartz , Mark Shulman , Mark Stephen Carney , Mark Whitford , Mark Y. Gilles , Mark Zangrilli , Marlyn C. Bautista , Marlyn C. Garcia , Marni Pont O'Doherty , Marsha A. Rodriguez , Marsha Dianah Ratchford , Martha Jane Stevens , Martha Reszke , Martin Boryczewski , Martin Coughlan , Martin DeMeo , Martin E. McWilliams , Martin Giovinazzo , Martin Lizzul , Martin Michael Wortley , Martin Morales Zempoaltecati , Martin Niederer , Martin P. Wohlforth , Martin Paul Michelstein , Marvin R. Woods , Mary (Molly) Herencia , Mary D. Stanley , Mary D'Antonio , Mary Ellen Tiesi , Mary Jane (MJ) Booth , Mary Jo Kimelman , Mary Katherine Boffa , Mary Kathleen Shearer , Mary Lenz Wieman , Mary Lou Hague , Mary Lou Langley , Mary Melendez , Mary Rubina Sperando , Mary S. Jones , Mary Teresa Caulfield , Mary Trentini , Mary Wahlstrom , Mary Yolanda Dowling , Masaru Ose , Matthew Barnes , Matthew Blake Wallens , Matthew Carmen Sellitto , Matthew D. Horning , Matthew David Garvey , Matthew David Yarnell , Matthew Diaz , Matthew Gerard Leonard , Matthew Gilbert Vianna , Matthew J. Burke , Matthew J. Grzymalski , Matthew Lancelot Ryan , Matthew Michael Flocco , Matthew Picerno , Matthew Rogan , Matthew T. McDermott , Matthew Timothy O'Mahony , Maureen L. Olson , Maurice Patrick Kelly , Maurice Vincent Barry , Mauricio Gonzalez , Maurita Tam , Maxima Jean-Pierre , Maynard S. Spence , Mayra Valdes-Rodriguez , Melanie Louise De Vere , Melissa C. Doi , Melissa Harrington Hughes , Melissa Rose Barnes , Melissa Vincent , Meredith Emily June Ewart , Meredith Lynn Whalen , Meta L. Waller , Michael A. Asciak , Michael A. Boccardi , Michael A. Marti , Michael A. Parkes , Michael A. Uliano , Michael Allen Davidson , Michael Allen Noeth , Michael Andrew Bane , Michael Andrew Tamuccio , Michael Anthony Tanner , Michael Beekman , Michael Benjamin Packer , Michael Boyle , Michael Bradley Finnegan , Michael C. Howell , Michael C. Opperman , Michael C. Sorresse , Michael C. Tarrou , Michael Cammarata , Michael Chung Ou , Michael Clarke , Michael Craig Rothberg , Michael Curtis Fiore , Michael D. D'Auria , Michael D. Mullan , Michael David Diehl , Michael David Ferugio , Michael DeRienzo , Michael Desmond McCarthy , Michael Diaz-Piedra , Michael E. Tinley , Michael Edward Asher , Michael Edward Gould , Michael Edward McHugh , Michael Edward Roberts , Michael Egan , Michael Emmett Brennan , Michael F. Lynch , Michael F. Stabile , Michael Francis Lynch , Michael G. Arczynski , Michael Gogliormella , Michael Grady Jacobs , Michael Gregory McGinty , Michael H. Waye , Michael Hardy Edwards , Michael Helmut Haub , Michael Horn , Michael J. Armstrong , Michael J. Berkeley , Michael J. Elferis , Michael J. Lyons , Michael J. McCabe , Michael J. Pascuma , Michael J. Pescherine , Michael James Stewart , Michael John Cahill , Michael John Simon , Michael Joseph Cawley , Michael Joseph Cunningham , Michael Joseph Duffy , Michael Joseph Mullin , Michael Joseph Zinzi , Michael Jude D'Esposito , Michael Kiefer , Michael L. Bocchino , Michael L. Collins , Michael L. DiAgostino , Michael L. Hannan , Michael L. Selves , Michael Lepore , Michael Lynch , Michael M. Taylor , Michael Massaroli , Michael Matthew Miller , Michael McDonnell , Michael Montesi , Michael O'Brien , Michael Otten , Michael P. Lunden , Michael Patrick Iken , Michael Patrick LaForte , Michael Patrick Tucker , Michael R. Canty , Michael R. Horrocks , Michael R. Wittenstein , Michael Ragusa , Michael Richards , Michael Roberts , Michael Rourke Andrews , Michael S. Baksh , Michael S. Costello , Michael Scott Carlo , Michael Seaman , Michael T. Carroll , Michael T. Wholey , Michael Taddonio , Michael Theodoridis , Michael Trinidad , Michael V. San Phillip , Michael W. Lomax , Michael W. Lowe , Michael Weinberg , Michel Adrian Pelletier , Michel Paris Colbert , Michele (Du Berry) Beale , Michele Ann Nelson , Michele B. Lanza , Michele Heidenberger , Michele L. Hoffmann , Michele Reed , Michell Lee Robotham , Michelle Coyle-Eulau , Michelle Herman Goldstein , Michelle Marie Henrique , Michelle Renee Bratton , Michelle Scarpitta , Michelle Titolo , Milagros "Millie" Hromada , Mildred Naiman , Milton Bustillo , Ming-Hao Liu , Mirna A. Duarte , Mitchel Scott Wallace , Mohammad Ali Sadeque , Mohammad Salman Hamdani , Mohammed Jawara , Mohammed Salahuddin Chowdhury , Mohammed Shajahan , Moira Smith , Moises N. Rivas , Molly McKenzie , Mon Gjonbalaj , Monica Goldstein , Monica Lyons , Monique E. DeJesus , Montgomery McCullough Hord , Morton Frank , Mukul Agarwala , Muriel F. Siskopoulos , Mychal Lamar Hulse , Myra Aronson , Myrna T. Maldonado-Agosto , Myrna Yaskulka , Myung-woo Lee , Nana Kwuku Danso , Nancy Bueche , Nancy Carole Farley , Nancy Diaz , Nancy E. Perez , Nancy Liz , Nancy Morgenstern , Nancy Muniz , Nancy T. Mauro , Nancy Yuen Ngo , Naomi Leah Solomon , Narender Nath , Nasima H. Simjee , Natalie Janis Lasden , Nathaniel Lawson , Nathaniel Webb , Nauka Kushitani , Neal Hinds , Nehamon Lyons , Neil D. Levin , Neil Dollard , Neil G. Shastri , Neil James Cudmore , Neil K. Leavy , Neil Leavy , Neil R. Wright , Neilie Anne Heffernan Casey , Nereida DeJesus , Nestor Andre Cintron , Nestor Chevalier , Nichola A. Thorpe , Nicholas A. Bogdan , Nicholas C. Lassman , Nicholas G. Massa , Nicholas Humber , Nicholas John , Nicholas P. Chiofalo , Nicholas P. Pietrunti , Nicholas P. Rossomando , Nicholas W. Brandemarti , Nick Rowe , Nickie L. Lindo , Nicole Miller , Nigel Bruce Thompson , Nilton Albuquerque Fernao Cunha , Nina Patrice Bell , Nitin Ramesh Parandkar , Niurka Davila , Nizam A. Hafiz , Nobuhiro Hayatsu , Noel J. Foster , Noell Maerz , Nolbert Salomon , Norbert P. Szurkowski , Norberto Hernandez , Norma C. Taddei , Norma Khan , Norma Lang Steuerle , Norman Rossinow , Nurul Huq Miah , Obdulio Ruiz Diaz , Odessa V. Morris , Olabisi L. Yee , Oleh D. Wengerchuk , Olga Kristin Gould White , Oliver Duncan Bennett , Orasri Liangthanasarn , Orio Joseph Palmer , Oscar de Laura , Oscar Nesbitt , Pablo Ortiz , Paige Farley-Hackel , Palmina Delli Gatti , Pamela Boyce , Pamela Chu , Pamela Gaff , Patrice Braut , Patrice Paz , Patricia A. Cody , Patricia A. Massari , Patricia A. McAneney , Patricia Ann Puma , Patricia Cushing , Patricia E. (Patti) Mickley , Patricia F. DiChiaro , Patricia J. Statz , Patricia Kuras , Patricia M. Fagan , Patricia Malia Colodner , Patricia Stanton , Patrick Adams , Patrick Aloysius Hoey , Patrick Byrne , Patrick Currivan , Patrick J. McGuire , Patrick J. O'Shea , Patrick James Buhse , Patrick Joseph Driscoll , Patrick Lyons , Patrick Michael Aranyos , Patrick O'Keefe , Patrick Quigley , Patrick Sean Murphy , Patrick Sullivan , Patrick Thomas Dwyer , Patrick W. Danahy , Patrick Woods , Paul A. Skrzypek , Paul A. Tegtmeier , Paul Ambrose , Paul Andrew Acquaviva , Paul Cascio , Paul Dario Curioli , Paul DeCola , Paul E. Jeffers , Paul F. Beatini , Paul F. Sarle , Paul Friedman , Paul G. Ruback , Paul Gary Bristow , Paul Hamilton Geier , Paul Hanlon Keating , Paul Innella , Paul James Battaglia , Paul James Furmato , Paul John Gill , Paul Joseph Simon , Paul K. Sloan , Paul Laszczynski , Paul Lisson , Paul M. Fiori , Paul Michael Benedetti , Paul Michael Beyer , Paul Ortiz , Paul Pansini , Paul R. Hughes , Paul R. Nimbley , Paul R. Salvio , Paul Rizza , Paul Robert Eckna , Paul Stuart Gilbey , Paul Talty , Paul W. Barbaro , Paul W. Jurgens , Paula Morales , Pauline Francis , Pedro (David) Grehan , Pedro Francisco Checo , Peggie Hurt , Pendyala Vamsikrishna , Perry Anthony Thompson , Pete Negron , Peter A. Chirchirillo , Peter A. Klein , Peter A. Siracuse , Peter Alexander Bielfeld , Peter Allen Nelson , Peter Anthony Vega , Peter Brennan , Peter C. Moutos , Peter Carroll , Peter Christian Fry , Peter Christopher Frank